erahtosis
bacteria of Tongue
germs
dry mouth
nervous
stuffy nose

MUSHROOM COOKERY

1. include mush last 10 minutes of cooking
2. saute + add before serving
3. avoid cooking more than 10 minutes

   mushroom watercress soup
   slice fine
   Bone in cup of chicken soup
   add watercress
   _____
   add to mushrooms

MUSHROOM COOKERY

ROSETTA REITZ

GRAMERCY PUBLISHING COMPANY
NEW YORK

for
Robin, Rebecca, and Rainbow

ACKNOWLEDGMENTS

I wish to express my thanks to Dr. Clark T. Rogerson, Curator, Cryptogamic Herbarium of the New York Botanical Gardens, for reading the chapter on wild mushrooms in manuscript, to the American Mushroom Institute for its cooperation, and to Susan Adams, its Home Economist and recipe consultant, particularly for her suggestion of the reversal of the egg white procedure in the mushroom soufflé.

My gratitude goes to William Cole, at whose suggestion I wrote this book and with whose helpful supervision it has become a reality, and to my sister Shelly, with whom I have had many very pleasant and detailed conversations about food in general and mushrooms in particular for years.

I am also indebted to Eileen and Bill Bowser for giving me my first taste of morels which they very carefully carried from Vermont. The greatest encouragement for clarity came from Joseph Mann, to whom I give my devoted thanks and appreciation. As a taster, he was a constant source of inspiration.

CONTENTS

MUSHROOM COOKERY

Introduction

Mushrooms are unique. They are delectable by themselves and they also enrich and enhance many other foods, without taking over. They are indispensable to fine cooking. All foods they are used with taste better: they give a distinctive flavor to sauces, soups, and stuffings; they make extraordinary hors d'oeuvres and first courses; and they can be either a garnish or a main dish. There is no getting around it—mushrooms are very important if you are seriously interested in food.

There are two distinct varieties of mushrooms: wild and cultivated. This book deals primarily with the cultivated variety. A chapter on the wild types has been included because these play a very special, if relatively minor, role in mushroom cookery.

All fresh mushrooms sold in supermarkets, produce markets, and groceries in the United States are cultivated. They are grown under precisely defined, scientific conditions and are the fruit of an edible fungus known botanically as *Agaricus campestris bisporus*. It takes about 60 days for a mushroom crop to mature for picking from the time the soil is prepared. Mushrooms are grown in mushroom beds about 7 inches deep. These beds, stacked in layers with about a foot of space between each, are in "mushroom houses" where heat, humidity, and light are very carefully controlled. Before the laboratory-prepared mushroom spawn is planted, the beds undergo a pasteurization, or "sweating out," process for a week at a temperature of 135° F. Mushroom pickers, or more accurately, cutters, wear miners' caps with lights on them when gathering the mushrooms for market.

The serious cultivation of mushrooms is not a new business. It goes back to the time of Louis XIV. Mushroom eating, however, dates from much earlier times. There were Chaldee words for edible mushrooms, and the Talmudic treatises refer to the blessing of mushrooms. Herodotus mentions the special vessels and forks used for eating them. Pliny referred to mushroom eaters as "dainty voluptuaries." The mushroom has had an irresistible fascination for centuries.

In our time many mushroom enthusiasts belong to special organizations. Some of these organizations are informal and some are scientific societies. But whether a member of an organization or not, a mushroom enthusiast is certain to be a devotee. I can't even remember when my devotion started; it's as though it were always there.

When I was nine years old I went to Europe with my mother and aunt and three large trunks. When we came back, the three trunks were empty of clothes, which had been given to friends, and stuffed full of dried mushrooms. It didn't seem the least bit strange to me. The mushrooms were ceps (*Boletus edulis*) strung on strings (the same mushrooms used in mushroom barley soup, and sold in supermarkets today in round plastic containers). They were presents brought back for friends, relatives, and neighbors. So much did we take it for granted that a string of dried wild mushrooms was the most desired gift from abroad that I've never wondered at my interest in them since. It was "natural."

It also seemed "natural" when I was asked to write a mushroom cookbook. It was something I always knew I'd do. I had been collecting, testing, and creating mushroom recipes for years. But once the project was underway the problem was one of selection. Not even all the classic dishes which require mushrooms could be included without making the book an encyclopedia.

Among the best known classics left out are Beef in Burgundy (*Boeuf Bourguignon*), Veal Stew with Cream (*Blanquette de Veau*), and Chicken in Red Wine (*Coq au Vin*). But there are reliable recipes for these dishes in many of the excellent cookbooks available today. However, it is important to point out that there are two correct methods of adding mushrooms to such main dishes. One is to include mushrooms only during the last 10 minutes of cooking and the other is to sauté the mushrooms and add them before serving. Avoid cooking mushrooms longer than 10 minutes, if possible.

Do Not Overcook Mushrooms

If they are used as important flavoring in a baked dish, be certain the mushrooms are sufficiently surrounded by other food so as to be protected from direct heat.

Don't wash or peel mushrooms. Wipe clean with fingers, or damp
16   *paper towel. Cut a thin slice off the bottom of each stem.*

Buying Mushrooms

The best mushrooms to buy are the freshest. These have closed caps and the gills on their undersides do not show. Fresh mushrooms are pure white, except for the brown strain variety which is available only on the West Coast. The tight, closed caps are firmer and heavier and are easier to slice, for the "skin" is more tender. As mushrooms mature (in a matter of days), they gradually lose moisture and open their caps. Frequently they shed spores from the gills, creating a very thin, brown layer, which looks like dust, on adjacent caps. This merely means that the mushrooms are ripening. In that condition they are perfectly good, usable, and full of flavor. Their fine taste is unimpaired.

Preparing Mushrooms for Cooking

DO NOT WASH. If there are specks of soil on the mushrooms, it is best to wipe them off with a damp towel. There is no danger of the gills being clogged with grit. Today mushrooms in the United States are always sent to market with closed caps. Caps open only after the mushrooms have left the distributor.

DO NOT PEEL. If a portion of a mushroom's surface does not look appealing, cut off only that spot and no more. The peel, or "skin," is a very flavorful element of a mushroom.

DO NOT SOAK. Mushrooms can easily become water-logged, and will lose vitamins, minerals, and flavor if they are immersed in water and left there. If you insist on washing them, do so by holding the mushrooms in your fingers, round side up, under cool running water for only a moment. Dry thoroughly. A damp towel will clean them most efficiently although, in most cases, just wiping them with the fingers is sufficient. Cut a thin slice off the bottom of each stem. This is where the mushrooms were cut in the mushroom house and this area sometimes becomes dry. However, when mushrooms are at their freshest even this cutting is not really necessary.

Storing Mushrooms

If mushrooms are to be used the day they are purchased, simply store them in the refrigerator in the bag or carton they were packed in. If there are some left to be used another day, place the mushrooms in an air-tight plastic container or bag before refrigerating. By the way, you will see the container developing beads of moisture after a couple of days; the mushrooms lose moisture as they mature. If mushrooms are purchased at their freshest, with closed, tight caps, they can be kept in the refrigerator for a full week and used as needed.

Bought in sufficient quantity (3 pounds), mushrooms often come in their own wooden basket for storage in the refrigerator. Be sure the mushrooms are completely covered with the basket lining paper. Lay two folded, well-dampened paper towels on top of the lining paper and cover, being careful to snap the wooden cover under the loops provided on the handle. This is the best way to keep mushrooms.

Cutting Mushrooms

Thinly sliced mushrooms are very commonly used in recipes, particularly in sauces. When sliced very fine, mushrooms give a lovely texture to the dish in which they are used. Slicing can be done very quickly on the large blade of a vegetable grater. Many

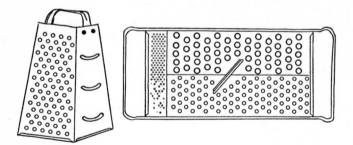

*Manufactured by Chief Products Co., 701 E. 59 St., Los Angeles, Calif.

18 *Don't wash or peel mushrooms. Wipe clean with fingers, or damp paper towel. Cut a thin slice off the bottom of each stem.*

kinds of graters with a large blade are available, including some attractive stainless steel ones imported from Sweden. But the one I like best for slicing mushrooms thin can usually be purchased in Woolworth chain stores and in some hardware stores. This fine utensil is called *All In One*.*

When sliced mushrooms are required, stems as well as caps are used. For finer chopping in half the time, slice mushrooms before chopping them.

Cooking Equipment for Mushrooms

The best pots and pans for cooking mushrooms are those made of stainless steel or enamelware. Aluminum may cause mushrooms to discolor. Heavy-bottomed pots are highly desirable because they distribute heat most evenly. The best size skillet for sautéeing one-half pound of sliced mushrooms or one pound of caps and stems (separated) is 12 inches in diameter.

Nutritive Value of Mushrooms

Although mushrooms contain quite a bit of moisture they are outstandingly nutritious. They are high in proteins, vitamins, and minerals. Proteins in mushrooms contain all of the eight amino acids known to be essential for human nutrition. Mushrooms are one of the finest natural sources for several vitamin B complex factors. They are exceptionally high in riboflavin (B_2) and thiamine (B_1). They are rich in niacin and pantothenic acid. Mushrooms also have a higher mineral content than that of most fruits and vegetables, particularly iron and copper.

Mushrooms and Calories

The most important thing to know about mushrooms and calories is:

there are only

66

calories in a pound.

Diets are dangerous unless they are strictly supervised by a physician, though fad diets keep turning up. But there are those times, particularly after holidays, vacations, or times of stress, when some people have added unwanted weight and want to "watch" or "cut down a little." Mushrooms are particularly good to include in the diet at such times, for instead of a deprivation, they seem almost like an indulgence. There are many recipes throughout this book which can help achieve that "cutting down." A broiled Mushroom Burger Simple is a good example. An average 1/4-pound hamburger has 300 calories. In the mushroom burger, half of the beef is replaced with mushrooms; the result is 167 calories—150 in the meat and 17 in the mushrooms. Mushroom Meat Loaf accomplishes the same thing.

Or have a first course of Mushroom Watercress Soup—only about 15 calories if you slice some mushrooms fine, boil them in a cup of chicken broth, and add watercress. This is delicious at any time.

Follow the directions for Stewed Mushrooms and keep them on hand in the refrigerator. Add some to the dishes you prepare. Be sure to check the Greens with Mushrooms. They are a particularly good calorie value, for half a cup of spinach, mustard greens, collards, or dandelion greens is only 12 1/2 calories and the mushrooms don't add too many more. You won't have to bother about the butter or bacon in those recipes because so little is actually used with a pound of greens.

If the sautéed mushrooms in the mashed potatoes recipe on page 116 are replaced with sliced, stewed ones, that becomes a good dish for calorie-counters; milk has already replaced butter. Baking powder and whipping expand a generous portion so that it looks like more than it really is, for potatoes are 78 percent water.

The red and white wine mushroom sauces are recommended to people who are "watching," for they allow plain broiled dishes to grow fancy at not very much calorie cost. These sauces are thickened with cornstarch, which is not only lower in calories than flour, but also binds a larger amount of liquid than the same quantity of flour will bind. The mushrooms in these sauces are boiled instead of sautéed, which means no butter is used. Although the recipes for these mushroom wine sauces do call for butter to be swirled in at

Don't wash or peel mushrooms. Wipe clean with fingers, or damp
20 *paper towel. Cut a thin slice off the bottom of each stem.*

the end, that step can be eliminated for calorie-cutting. Mushroom Spaghetti Sauce is not a fattening sauce either. Instead of using it on spaghetti, trim down by using it spooned over chicken, fish, or meat.

Especially good, and low in calories, is the Mushroom Cottage Cheese Sauce. This high-protein sauce will make dishes seem like party ones rather than weight-watching ones. Use lavishly on asparagus, broccoli, broiled fish, eggs, or a tossed green saled.

The cook who masters the art of using mushrooms will turn out fine dishes with an ease once thought to require the special skill of a great chef. Mushrooms have long been referred to as food for the gods. It is the purpose of MUSHROOM COOKERY to demonstrate that the average home cook, with a modicum of care and practice, can produce divine meals. Proceed.

Hors d'oeuvres

MARINATED MUSHROOMS

¾ of a quart

Marinated mushrooms, commonly called mushrooms à la Grecque, make a cocktail tray luxurious. Served on lettuce leaves they can be either a first course or a salad. Or they can be sliced into a green salad, or be part of an antipasto. Flute them before cooking if you want to use them for a fancy garnish on cold platters. They can be kept in the refrigerator for 2 weeks.

1 lb. mushrooms	½ tsp. oregano
¼ cup olive oil	1 Tbsp. dried parsley
½ cup corn oil	1 Tbsp. dry mustard
¼ cup wine vinegar	1 tsp. salt
2 bay leaves	¼ tsp. pepper
1 tsp. chervil	2 Tbsp. dry wine

Place all ingredients, except mushrooms and wine, in a large pot. Bring this marinade to a boil. Add mushrooms (whole). Shake the pot and stir the liquid to be sure all mushrooms are moistened.

Cover and cook over moderate heat for 5 minutes.

Rinse a quart glass jar with very hot water and let it drain. Remove the pot from the heat and spoon mushrooms into the jar with a perforated spoon. Allow mushrooms to cool in the jar for half an hour, uncovered. Let the marinade cool in the pot. It may or may not be strained. Pour cooled marinade over mushrooms. Add wine. Cover and refrigerate.

Don't wash or peel mushrooms. Wipe clean with fingers, or damp
paper towel. Cut a thin slice off the bottom of each stem.

MUSHROOM DEVILED EGGS

16 deviled egg halves

Mushrooms go with eggs. These deviled eggs make a fine lunch, are attractive as garnish on cold platters, and are particularly good as hors d'oeuvres. The flavor is subtle, but certain.

1/4 lb. mushrooms	2 Tbsp. mayonnaise
2 Tbsp. onion chopped fine	2 Tbsp. prepared mustard
2 Tbsp. butter	1 Tbsp. lemon juice
8 hard-cooked eggs	1/2 tsp. celery salt
1/8 tsp. white pepper	

Shred 1/4 pound of mushrooms, then chop a little. Sauté them with 2 tablespoons of finely chopped onion in a large skillet in 2 tablespoons of butter for 3 minutes.

Cut the eggs in half and remove the yolks. Mash the yolks with 2 tablespoons each of mayonnaise and prepared mustard, 1 tablespoon of lemon juice, 1/2 teaspoon of celery salt, and 1/8 teaspoon of white pepper. Work the yolks into a smooth paste, add the mushrooms, and mix well.

Fill the whites with this mixture. If you use a spoon for filling them, smooth the mounds with a knife. A large star tube in a pastry bag does a good, quick job of filling the 16 egg-white halves attractively. Garnish the top of each with a small marinated button mushroom or a sautéed mushroom cap.

EGG MUSHROOM SPREAD

Serves 6

½ lb. mushrooms
4 Tbsp. softened butter
1 medium onion

6 hard-cooked eggs
1 tsp. salt
⅛ tsp. pepper

Shred ½ pound of mushrooms and chop a little. Sauté them in 2 tablespoons of butter in a large skillet for 5 minutes, stirring from time to time. Transfer to a large bowl.

Grate onion over the mushrooms. Hook a medium-size strainer over the bowl and, with a tablespoon, force 6 hard-cooked eggs through the strainer. Sliced eggs force more easily.

Add 1 teaspoon of salt, ⅛ teaspoon of pepper, and the remaining 2 tablespoons of butter. Mix thoroughly and chill.

Scoop onto lettuce leaves for a first course, or serve as a spread, surrounded with unsalted crackers or toast triangles.

Don't wash or peel mushrooms. Wipe clean with fingers, or damp paper towel. Cut a thin slice off the bottom of each stem.

CREAM CHEESE MUSHROOM SPREAD

¾ cup spread

1/4 lb. mushrooms
3 oz. cream cheese
2 Tbsp. butter

Shred and chop mushrooms. Heat 2 tablespoons of butter in a skillet until bubbling. Add the mushrooms. Cook for 4 or 5 minutes over moderately high heat, stirring frequently to allow steam to escape. Remove to a plate to cool.

Have a 3-ounce package of cream cheese at room temperature in a bowl. Whip it with a fork for about 2 minutes to make it fluffy. Add the cooled mushrooms and blend them in thoroughly.

If this spread is going to be served with salty cocktail crackers it should be used as is. If it is to be used for thin sandwiches, add salt and pepper to taste.

Any amount of cream cheese from 3 to 8 ounces may be creamed with 1/4 pound of mushrooms prepared in this manner.

MUSHROOM CHIPS

It is best to use large, firm mushrooms with closed caps for this dish. They make large slices. Even with the shrinkage that occurs, 1/2 pound of mushrooms yields enough chips to fill a quart bowl.

1/2 to 1 lb. mushrooms
1 cup oil
salt

————————••◀∞▶••————————

Heat I cup of oil in a 11/2- or 2-quart saucepan to 375°. Use a frying basket or perforated spoon for removing the chips from the oil.

Have the mushrooms at room temperature. Cold ones will cause the temperature of the fat to drop too quickly. Slice the mushrooms thin on the large blade of a vegetable grater.

To begin, drop some slices singly into the fat. They will start to brown and curl within 2 minutes. When browned, remove them to paper towels and sprinkle with salt. Drop a handful in next and stir with a fork to be sure they separate. When curled and browned remove to paper towels for draining. Salt them.

Continue frying a handful at a time. No more or they'll stick together. These are best served as soon as they're made, but they can be prepared in advance. Although they're good cold, they're crisper if heated on a cookie tin before serving.

Don't wash or peel mushrooms. Wipe clean with fingers, or damp
paper towel. Cut a thin slice off the bottom of each stem.

NUTTY MUSHROOM BALLS

About 40 balls the size of large marbles

1/4 lb. mushrooms
1/2 lb. soft cheddar cheese
1 Tbsp. brandy
1/4 lb. salted peanuts

————————◄∞►————————

Leave 1/2 pound of soft cheddar cheese at room temperature for a few hours before creaming it. It will handle more easily. In a bowl soften the cheese further by pouring a tablespoon of brandy over it and whip it to make it fluffy.

Slice 1/4 pound of mushrooms on the large blade of a vegetable grater, then chop. Add the mushrooms to the cheese and mix well.

Chop the peanuts. This is most easily done by pouring them into an electric blender and turning it on and off at lowest speed. Move the top nuts to the bottom and turn on and off again.

Spread the nuts on a piece of wax paper. Spoon out 1/2 teaspoonful of the mushroom-cheese paste onto the nuts and roll it, covering with nuts. Shape the balls more firmly by rolling between the palms of your hands. Place on a flat platter or pan lined with wax paper. Chill for at least 3 hours before serving.

MUSHROOMS IN BATTER

15 to 20 caps in batter

When these are passed around, even the most exciting conversations stop. Have a small fork and paper napkins on the tray; toothpicks are inadequate.

1 lb. mushrooms	1/8 tsp. pepper
1/2 cup milk (scant)	1/2 tsp. onion powder
1 egg	1/2 tsp. celery salt
1/2 cup flour	1/8 tsp. nutmeg
1/2 tsp. baking powder	dash of cayenne
3/4 tsp. salt	1 tsp. angostura bitters

1 cup oil

--------◦◦◦◦--------

Cut the stems from 1 pound of mushrooms 1/4 inch away from the caps. Stems hold the batter better than the gills and also supply the mushrooms with their own pedestals on the serving tray.

Mix all ingredients, except the mushrooms and the oil, in a bowl. Beat the batter well.

Heat a cup of oil in a saucepan to 375°.

Work with only 6 mushrooms at a time. Drop them into the batter, using two tablespoons to coat the mushrooms. Slip a battered mushroom, round side down, into the hot oil. Continue until the 6 caps are in the oil. The first one will then be brown enough to turn over. Turn the others. When the caps are brown on both sides, remove them with a perforated spoon and drain the mushrooms on paper towels. Repeat until all the mushrooms are used. The stems can be battered in the hot oil too. Be careful not to cook too many at once. Separate them from each other with a fork. Serve surrounded with parsley.

Don't wash or peel mushrooms. Wipe clean with fingers, or damp
paper towel. Cut a thin slice off the bottom of each stem.

PÂTÉ OF PORK AND MUSHROOMS

This pâté can be kept in the refrigerator for two weeks if it is wrapped in airtight metal foil.

3/4 lb. mushrooms
1 lb. pork liver
1/2 lb. pork
7 bacon strips
1 egg
1 medium onion sliced

2 sprigs parsley
1 Tbsp. flour
1/4 tsp. thyme
1/4 tsp. allspice
1/4 tsp. cinnamon
1/2 tsp. salt
1/8 tsp. pepper

Remove the stems from 3/4 pound of mushrooms. Remove the outer membranes and tubes from 1 pound of pork liver and cut into 1-inch strips. Roughly dice 1/2 pound of uncooked pork and 2 strips of bacon.

Blend all the ingredients listed except the mushroom caps and the 5 strips of bacon in an electric blender. This will require three separate blendings. In a large bowl mix all the purée together well.

Line the bottom of a standard meat loaf or bread pan, 9 x 5 x 3, with 2 strips of bacon. Turn out 1/3 of the mixture onto the bacon. On this lay 1/2 of the mushroom caps, round side up. Add another 1/3 of the mixture and use the remaining caps. Fill with the rest of the liver purée.

Arrange the remaining 3 slices of bacon along the top. Cover with a piece of tightly fitting metal foil. Place in a pan of hot water so that one-half the depth of the pâté pan is in the water. Bake in a preheated 400° oven for 1 1/2 hours.

Remove from the oven and test for doneness by inserting a metal knife into the pâté. It should come out clean. If it doesn't, cover and return to the oven without the water for 10 more minutes.

Cool at room temperature before refrigerating. Serve chilled.

MUSHROOM TOAST

32 hot hors d'oeuvres

½ lb. mushrooms
  1 can water chestnuts (5 oz.)
  1 medium onion
  2 tsp. salt
  1 tsp. sugar

1 tsp. monosodium glutamate
1 Tbsp. cornstarch
1 egg
8 slices white bread
  bread crumbs

1 cup oil

Drain water chestnuts and dry them on paper towels. Chop and place in a large bowl.

Grate 1 medium onion over the chestnuts.

Shred ½ pound of mushrooms and chop a little. Add them to the bowl, along with 2 teaspoons of salt, 1 teaspoon of sugar, 1 teaspoon of m.s.g., 1 tablespoon of cornstarch, and 1 egg. Mix very well.

Trim the crusts from 8 slices of bread. Spread the mushroom mixture on each slice and cut into 4 triangles. Sprinkle with bread crumbs.

Heat 1 cup of oil in a skillet to 375° and place the triangles in hot fat, mushroom side down. Brown and turn. Drain on paper towels and serve garnished with parsley.

Don't wash or peel mushrooms. Wipe clean with fingers, or damp
paper towel. Cut a thin slice off the bottom of each stem.

DAIRY LIVER

6 servings as first course

Dairy liver is a New York City food phenomenon that appears on menus of dairy restaurants which do not serve meat. It is a "mock" chopped liver, substituting mushrooms for liver. So why not call it chopped mushrooms? They don't. But it tastes good, even with the wrong name.

1 lb. mushrooms	*2 hard-cooked eggs*
4 Tbsp. oil	*1 tsp. salt*
1 large onion sliced	*⅛ tsp. pepper*

Chop fine or grind 1 pound of mushrooms and 1 onion sliced in a meat grinder, using the finest blade.

Sauté half of the mushroom-onion mixture in 2 tablespoons of oil for about 5 minutes, stirring from time to time. Remove to a bowl and sauté the remaining half in 2 more tablespoons of oil in the same way.

Chop 2 hard-cooked eggs and add them with 1 teaspoon of salt and ⅛ teaspoon of pepper to the mushrooms. Mix well and chill.

Serve as a first course on lettuce leaves, or as a cocktail spread.

CALF'S LIVER PÂTÉ

About 2½ cups

Mushrooms give this pâté a lightness it lacks otherwise. The whole caps embedded in it make the pâté slices very attractive.

¾ lb. mushrooms	1 cup chicken broth
½ lb. calf's liver	3 sprigs parsley
2 Tbsp. butter	¼ tsp. tarragon
1 Tbsp. oil	¼ tsp. dill weed
1 small onion sliced	1 tsp. salt
1 Tbsp. brandy	⅛ tsp. pepper

1 Tbsp. gelatin (1 env.)

Remove the outer membranes and tubes from the liver. Cut it into one inch strips and sauté in 2 tablespoons of butter and 1 tablespoon of oil in a large skillet. Sauté for 3 minutes on both sides. The liver should be medium rare. Remove the liver to the jar of an electric blender. Spoon out the froth substance from the skillet, leaving the fat.

Separate the caps from the stems of ¾ of a pound of mushrooms. Place them, along with 1 small sliced onion, into the skillet. Add 1 tablespoon of brandy, cover and steam for 5 minutes. Remove 10 caps and reserve.

Pour ¼ cup of chicken broth over the liver in the blender and turn it on at high speed for ½ minute. Add another ¼ cup of the broth and the steamed mushrooms and onions from the skillet, 3 sprigs of parsley, ¼ teaspoon each of tarragon and dill, a teaspoon of salt, and ⅛ teaspoon of pepper. Blend well.

Pour the remaining ½ cup of broth in a small saucepan. Sprinkle 1 tablespoon of gelatin over it. After it has softened, heat to dissolve the gelatin. Add this to the liver mixture in the blender and blend again.

In a 2½-cup mold pour ⅓ of the pâté. On this place 5 of the

34 *Don't wash or peel mushrooms. Wipe clean with fingers, or damp paper towel. Cut a thin slice off the bottom of each stem.*

reserved mushroom caps, round side down. Add another $1/3$ of the pâté and use the remaining 5 caps in the same way. Pour the balance of the liver mixture over the caps and smooth the top with a knife. Chill overnight. Unmold the next day and surround with greens.

HAM ROLLS

16 ham rolls

$1/4$ lb. mushrooms
$1/2$ lb. boiled ham, 16 thin
   slices

1 Tbsp. lemon juice
2 Tbsp. olive oil
$1/4$ tsp. salt
$1/4$ tsp. powdered cardamon

Slice $1/4$ pound of mushrooms fine on the large blade of a vegetable grater. Place the slices in a bowl and sprinkle with 1 tablespoon of lemon juice, 2 tablespoons of oil, and $1/4$ teaspoon each of salt and cardamon. Mix well.

Lay the ham slices out. Place a generous tablespoon of the mixture on the lower third of each ham slice. Fold up from the bottom and fold each end in toward the center. Roll until the ham is used. Chill for at least one hour before serving.

STUFFED MUSHROOMS

Stuffed mushrooms can be used in a number of ways. They can be hors d'oeuvres, platter garnishes, the first course, the vegetable, or even the main course. The choice of fillings depends upon the cook's taste and imagination. The range extends from corn-meal mush to fresh Molossol caviar.

As a breakfast dish, a large mushroom cap can be an interesting vehicle in which to poach an egg. For lunch, a boiled cap can house a shrimp salad. Use the recipe for Basic Baked Stuffed Mushrooms for the cocktail tray or as a first course. Stuff some caps with finely chopped spinach mixed with some bread crumbs and bake in cream for a unique vegetable. Follow the directions for Mushroom Meat Loaf and stuff caps with it for a main dish.

The variety is endless. The following list is intended merely to act as a stimulus for your own invention:

liver	oysters	spinach
tongue	crab meat	eggs
hamburger	pâtés	anchovies
sausage (cooked)	fish	capers
shrimp	chicken	caviar
snails	turkey	olives
clams	ham	avocado
cheeses (from cream cheese to sharp cheddar)	lobster	nuts

Stuffing must not be dry or it will fall apart, but it must not be soggy either. It must "handle well" as you place it into the cap.

Do not cut mushroom stems to remove them for stuffing, snap them to one side instead. This provides a depression in the center of the cap.

If possible, buy large mushrooms for stuffing. They may run from 12 to 20 to a pound. Very fresh, firm closed caps are heavier than open-capped mushrooms with the gills showing. Open caps

Don't wash or peel mushrooms. Wipe clean with fingers, or damp
36 *paper towel. Cut a thin slice off the bottom of each stem.*

have lost moisture and are lighter in weight. They don't look quite as pretty, but they taste fine.

Some people prefer serving stuffed mushrooms after they have "rested" at room temperature. They are good either way.

There are four ways of preparing mushrooms to be stuffed: baking, boiling, broiling, and sautéeing.

BAKED MUSHROOMS

This is an easy method. Neither the caps nor the stems have to be cooked before baking. The mushrooms cook during the baking. Many cooks sauté the stems first but this adds unnecessary fat to the stuffing. The moisture in the stems is released during the 15-minute baking period; this adds succulence. To reduce the raw taste of chopped onions, shallots, or scallions, some cooks like to sauté them before they are added. However, if they are grated they automatically lose their raw taste during the baking time, and also add additional moisture, without extra fat. The concern with fat is to avoid a greasy taste, for it can overpower the delicacy of the mushroom, particularly when the mushrooms are no longer hot.

The following recipe for baked stuffed mushrooms is a good basic one. Use it as is or use it to elaborate on by adding 1/2 cup of cooked food, such as chopped shrimp or ham. No change is necessary, for the interior moisture is provided by the chopped stems and grated onion. The shredded cheese acts as a binder.

Baked stuffed mushrooms can be prepared in advance up to the point of baking. If they are stored in the refrigerator, they should be brought to room temperature before baking.

BASIC BAKED STUFFED MUSHROOMS

1 lb. large mushrooms	1/2 tsp. salt
oil	pepper
1/2 cup fine bread crumbs	2 Tbsp. (or more) milk,
1/2 cup finely shredded	cream, or stock
Gruyère or Swiss cheese	bread crumbs
4 Tbsp. grated onion and	Parmesan or Romano
juice	cheese, grated
1/2 tsp. chervil or tarragon	butter

Remove the stems from 1 pound of large mushrooms.

Pour some oil into a bowl. With your fingers wipe some oil over the outside of each cap. Add a drop in the center of the inside, too, but don't add more oil once the first has become absorbed. Chop the stems fine, or use the easier technique of shredding them first and then chopping.

In a bowl combine the chopped mushrooms with 1/2 cup fine bread crumbs by tossing together with a fork. Add 1/2 cup finely shredded Gruyère or Swiss cheese and toss some more. Add 4 tablespoons of grated onion and onion juice, 1/2 teaspoon of chervil or tarragon, 1/2 teaspoon of salt, and several turns of the pepper mill. Toss with fork again and add 2 tablespoons of milk, cream, or stock. A little more may be needed to make the mixture moist enough so it holds together and doesn't crumble apart when it is handled.

Stuff the caps with the mixture. Round and smooth with your fingers. Sprinkle each cap with some bread crumbs and some grated Parmesan or Romano cheese, and dot each one with butter. Place the caps in a baking pan and bake in a preheated 375° oven for 15 minutes. If the caps are very large and heavy give them a couple of additional minutes baking time.

Baked mushrooms may be buttered instead of oiled. They may also be baked without being oiled or buttered if there is 1/2 inch of

Don't wash or peel mushrooms. Wipe clean with fingers, or damp
38   *paper towel. Cut a thin slice off the bottom of each stem.*

moisture in the baking pan. It can be milk, cream, stock, or sauce. The mushrooms must not be allowed to dry out.

Boiled Mushrooms

Boiled caps are best for chilled stuffed mushrooms. They should be boiled in lemon water for 5 minutes and removed from the liquid immediately. Follow the directions for Stewed Mushrooms (see Index).

The advantage in using boiled mushrooms for stuffing is that they can be completely prepared in advance. They also lend themselves to elaborate garnishes, such as diamond-shaped truffles and petals cut from red pimento. Or they may be covered with aspic.

Cold stuffed mushrooms can be filled with cold salads, such as lobster, shrimp, crab meat, tuna, egg, ham, tongue, etc. The stems should be boiled with the caps and chopped into the salads too. Serve clams or oysters in an uncommon way by placing them on boiled caps. Before adding the shellfish, place a spoon of cocktail sauce in the depression in the cap. Then garnish the top with a slice of lemon.

Another attractive hors d'oeuvre uses liver pâté. Soften a can of pâté with a tablespoon of brandy, fold some whipped cream into it to make it fluffy, and pile this onto a cold boiled mushroom cap. Garnish with a piece of truffle. If it happens to be a poor truffle year, or you don't happen to have some handy, a similar *appearance* can be achieved by using black olives. An efficient and beautiful way to stuff cold mushroom caps is to force the filling through a pastry bag with a many-pointed tube.

Broiled Mushrooms

Remove the stems from the mushrooms. Pour some oil in a bowl and, using your fingers, oil the caps (or use softened butter if you prefer). Place the caps, round side up, under a preheated broiler, but not too close to the heat, about 3 or 4 inches away, and broil for 2 minutes. Turn the caps and broil the undersides for 2 minutes.

Remove from heat and stuff them. Dot the tops with butter and broil again for about 4 minutes. They are ready when they begin to brown.

Remember, when broiling stuffed mushrooms, that the mixture doesn't cook very long. Therefore don't use ingredients which require more than 4 minutes broiling time.

The chief advantage of broiling stuffed mushrooms is they're quick. One of the best stuffings is Mushroom Duxelles (see Index). Combine duxelles with the same amount of bread crumbs and moisten for easy handling. They're fabulous.

Sautéed Mushrooms

To sauté mushroom caps as preparation for stuffing is the least practical of the four methods. If the stuffed mushrooms are to be baked, they don't need to be sautéed first. If they are to be broiled, the caps can be broiled too. The only way sautéeing caps makes sense is if the stuffing is cooked in the caps in the skillet. The caps can be sautéed in advance, stuffed, and stored to be broiled just before serving. But then, the caps may as well have been broiled first too—it's faster.

Soup

MUSHROOM SOUPS

Soups taste better with mushrooms in them. Any soup can be transformed into a mushroom soup simply by adding mushrooms and cooking for only 5 minutes. If the mushrooms are sliced fine, which is easily done by using the large blade of a vegetable grater (see Introduction), they will float throughout the soup.

Space limits the number of soup recipes which can be given. But make up your own by adding mushrooms to your favorite soups. If you have lentils, beans, rice, potatoes, or any green vegetables left over, add them to stock or broth and cook with some mushrooms.

MUSHROOM CHICKEN BROTH

2 to 3 servings

1/4 lb. mushrooms
2 cups chicken broth
fresh chopped parsley

Slice 1/4 pound of mushrooms fine on the large blade of a vegetable grater. Cook them in 2 cups of chicken broth for 5 minutes. Sprinkle with fresh chopped parsley.

MUSHROOM WATERCRESS SOUP

2 to 3 servings

Prepare the preceding recipe for Mushroom Chicken Broth and before serving, add a handful of watercress, with stems removed, to the soup pot. Stir. The watercress should be wilted, not cooked.

YOGURT MUSHROOM SOUP

2 to 3 servings

This is a lovely sour soup and is especially refreshing served hot for summer menus. Prepare the recipe for Mushroom Chicken Broth and before serving, spoon $1/2$ cup of yogurt into the soup. The yogurt should not be cooked.

CREAM OF MUSHROOM SOUP

4 to 6 servings

This is a pure mushroom cream soup which glorifies the mushrooms in it. Add 2 more cups of milk to Basic Mushroom Sauce I (see Index) to make it. Spoon a teaspoon of butter into each bowl before serving. For a richer soup, replace some of the milk with cream.

CREAM OF WHEAT MUSHROOM SOUP

6 servings

This is really a fancy porridge. It is a delightful change for breakfast. It's also one of those soups to have when you're not feeling well, but want something more than plain broth.

Follow the directions on a package of Cream of Wheat for four servings. When the Cream of Wheat is cooked, add it to the preceding recipe for Cream of Mushroom Soup.

Don't wash or peel mushrooms. Wipe clean with fingers, or damp
paper towel. Cut a thin slice off the bottom of each stem.

MUSHROOM CHOWDER

6 servings

Mushroom Chowder is delicious as is. It can be enriched by adding fish or shellfish. If quahogs are used, remove the muscle, chop them fine, and add to the pot along with the potatoes. Smaller, more tender clams or oysters should be added with the mushrooms. Lobster or crab meat should be added with the cooked bacon and need only be thoroughly heated.

        1 lb. mushrooms
        4 slices bacon
        1 large onion, chopped
        2 cups potatoes, diced small
        2 cups water
    $1/2$ tsp. salt
    $1/8$ tsp. black pepper
        2 Tbsp. butter
           light cream (1 to 2 cups)

Cut 4 slices of bacon into $1/4$-inch strips. Render it in a large pot until the pieces are brown. Remove them to a paper towel to drain.

Sauté 1 large chopped onion in the bacon fat until it is golden but not brown. Pour off half the fat and discard. Add 2 cups of potatoes cut into $1/2$-inch dice, 2 cups of water, $1/2$ teaspoon of salt, and $1/8$ teaspoon of black pepper. Boil covered for 30 minutes.

Cut 1 pound of mushrooms into quarters and add to the pot with 2 cups of milk. Simmer slowly for 10 minutes. Return the bacon pieces. Swirl in 2 tablespoons of butter and pour 1 cup or more of light cream into the soup. Taste for salt.

GAZPACHO

1 quart gazpacho

This cold Spanish soup is becoming an American favorite, appearing more and more frequently on summer menus. Gazpacho is sometimes called a liquid salad and can in fact become a salad when it is chilled in aspic (see Index for Gazpacho Aspic).

1/4 lb. mushrooms	4 scallions
2 1/2 cups canned multiple vegetable juice	2 cloves garlic
3 Tbsp. lemon juice	1/3 cup olive oil
2 tomatoes	1 tsp. salt
1 cucumber	1/8 tsp. pepper
1/2 green pepper	2 Tbsp. fresh chopped parsley

Tabasco

In a large bowl combine 2 1/2 cups of canned multiple vegetable juice with 3 tablespoons of lemon juice.

Slice 1/4 pound of mushrooms fine on the large blade of a vegetable grater. Add them to the juices and stir carefully to be sure all of the mushroom slices are separated and coated with juice. This will preserve their color.

Chop fine: 2 tomatoes, a cucumber, 1/2 green pepper and 4 scallions, including some of the green, and add to the bowl. Mince 2 cloves of garlic and add, along with 1/3 cup of olive oil, 1 teaspoon of salt, 1/8 teaspoon of freshly ground black pepper, 2 tablespoons of fresh chopped parsley, and 2 dashes of Tabasco sauce. Mix everything well and chill.

Taste the gazpacho for seasoning after it is thoroughly chilled. It may need more salt, or if you like it snappier, add another dash or two of Tabasco. Serve in individual chilled glass bowls with an ice cube in the center of each bowl. This cold soup improves in flavor if kept in the refrigerator for a few days.

Don't wash or peel mushrooms. Wipe clean with fingers, or damp
46 *paper towel. Cut a thin slice off the bottom of each stem.*

MUSHROOM POTATO SOUP

10 to 12 servings

Mushroom potato soup is served hot. Served chilled, it becomes Mushroom Vichyssoise.

1 lb. mushrooms
4 leeks (or 2 medium onions)
1 medium onion
2 Tbsp. butter

3 cups raw potatoes, small
  dice
4 cups chicken broth
  milk or cream

—————••◦◦◦••—————

Trim the roots and green tops from 4 leeks. Cut the leeks in half, the long way, and wash well under running water. Be sure to get all the sand out. Cut the leeks in $1/2$-inch slices; there should be about 2 cups. Peel and chop, not too fine, 1 medium onion. (If onions are substituted for leeks, chop 3 onions.)

Melt 2 tablespoons of butter in a 4-quart pot and cook the leeks and onions slowly, for 5 minutes, covered, stirring from time to time.

Add 3 cups of diced potatoes and 4 cups of chicken broth. Cover and simmer the soup for 25 minutes. Add 1 pound of whole mushrooms and simmer, covered, for 10 more minutes.

Pour 2 cups of soup into an electric blender and blend for about a minute, using highest speed. Add another cup and blend some more. Continue until all the soup is blended. The blender will have to be emptied three times.

After blending, there will be 2 quarts of thick soup. This will have to be thinned down to serve. It can be kept in the refrigerator longer if it is stored before adding milk or cream. This soup freezes well and if some is to be frozen, it is best to do it at this point, before thinning it down.

To prepare 4 servings, heat 3 cups of blended soup with 1 cup of milk or cream and slowly bring it to a boil. Remove from heat. If a thinner soup is desired, add more milk or cream. Store or freeze the rest.

MUSHROOM VICHYSSOISE

Follow the preceding recipe for Mushroom Potato Soup. After adding the milk or cream, chill for at least 3 hours. Before serving, stir 2 tablespoons of chilled heavy cream into each bowl.

CZECH MUSHROOM SOUP

8 to 12 servings

This is a thick peasant soup and makes one think of hard work and cold weather. Caraway seeds add a snappy taste. For a thinner soup, add milk at the end.

1/2 lb. mushrooms	4 Tbsp. flour
1 qt. water	2 pts. sour cream
4 medium to large potatoes, diced	1 tsp. dry dill weed or 1 Tbsp. fresh dill
1 tsp. caraway seeds	1/8 tsp. black pepper
2 tsp. salt	2 eggs

———————— ⋅∞⋅ ————————

Pour a quart of water into a 3- or 4-quart pot and add a teaspoon of caraway seeds and 2 teaspoons of salt. Boil 4 diced potatoes in it for 15 minutes, covered.

Stir 4 tablespoons of flour into 2 pints of sour cream and mix thoroughly. Stir this into the potato pot. Don't worry if it curdles— it will smooth out.

Slice the mushrooms thick and add them. Cover and simmer for 10 minutes. Turn the heat off. Sprinkle with a tablespoon of fresh dill or a teaspoon of dry dill weed and 1/8 teaspoon of freshly ground coarse black pepper.

In a small bowl beat 2 eggs and spoon some hot soup over them. Stir. Add a little more soup and pour this egg mixture into the soup pot and stir some more.

Don't wash or peel mushrooms. Wipe clean with fingers, or damp paper towel. Cut a thin slice off the bottom of each stem.

MUSHROOM MADRILENE
(Jellied Mushroom Soup)
4 servings

1/2 lb. mushrooms
1 Tbsp. unflavored gelatin
    (1 envelope)
2 1/4 cups beef stock
2 Tbsp. lemon juice
1/2 tsp. tarragon
1/2 tsp. salt
    pepper
2 Tbsp. tomato paste
2 Tbsp. red wine
1 crushed egg shell
4 tsp. sherry

————————•◦∞◦•————————

Slice 1/2 pound of mushrooms fine on the large blade of a vegetable grater.

Pour 1/2 cup of cool beef stock in a saucepan. Soften 1 tablespoon of gelatin in it. Pour 1 3/4 cups more beef stock into the saucepan and bring to a boil. Add 2 tablespoons of lemon juice, 1/2 teaspoon each of tarragon and salt, and a few turns of the pepper mill. Add the sliced mushrooms. Cover and boil moderately for 5 minutes. Remove mushroom slices with a perforated spoon to a bowl. Cover and reserve.

To the boiled beef stock add 2 tablespoons of tomato paste, 2 tablespoons of red wine, and a crushed egg shell. Bring to a boil. Remove from heat and let it rest for 10 minutes. Line a paper towel in a medium-size strainer. Hook it onto a bowl and pour the stock through the strainer. Chill until it begins to thicken. It should have the consistency of unbeaten egg whites. Fold in the mushroom slices and chill for one more hour.

Sprinkle each serving with 1 teaspoon of sherry. Garnish with chopped parsley and lemon slices.

MUSHROOM MATZO BALLS

12 matzo balls

By any other name, such as dumplings or knoedel, they taste as good. Matzo balls are served in chicken broth. They can also be baked and served with the main course in place of a starch.

1/4 lb. mushrooms	1/8 tsp. white pepper
4 eggs	1/3 cup melted shortening
1/2 cup water	1 Tbsp. lemon juice
1 tsp. salt	1 cup matzo meal*

In a 2- or 3-quart bowl, using a wire whisk, beat 4 eggs with 1/2 cup of water, a teaspoon of salt and 1/8 teaspoon of pepper.

Add 1/3 cup of melted shortening and mix well. (The best shortening for this dish is rendered chicken fat. Oil, melted butter, or melted bacon fat may also be used.) Add a tablespoon of lemon juice.

Chop fine or shred 1/4 pound of mushrooms on a vegetable grater and mix them into the egg-fat mixture. Add a cup of matzo meal and mix again. Allow it to rest for 20 minutes.

In a 3- or 4-quart pot bring 1 1/2 quarts of water or chicken broth to a rolling boil. (Add a tablespoon of salt if water is used.) Shape the mixture into 12 large balls. This is most neatly done with cool wet hands. After shaping, drop each matzo ball into the vigorously boiling liquid. When the mixture is all used, turn the heat down a little. Boil the matzo balls for 15 minutes uncovered. Serve them in chicken broth, 1 or 2 in each bowl.

To bake: remove from the cooking liquid with a perforated spoon and drain on paper towels. Pat matzo balls dry. Roast uncovered in a baking dish, dotting each with butter, for 30 minutes in a preheated 450° oven.

*Some supermarkets place matzo meal next to breadcrumbs, others place it next to matzos.

Don't wash or peel mushrooms. Wipe clean with fingers, or damp paper towel. Cut a thin slice off the bottom of each stem.

MUSHROOM BARLEY SOUP

There are many myths about mushroom barley soup and they all have one thing in common—the soup makes the eater wise. Well . . . who knows about food and wisdom? But the eater does know the soup tastes good.

There are two kinds of mushroom barley soup. One is a milk soup and the other is a stock soup made with meat. Dried and fresh mushrooms are used in both the recipes. These soups freeze well.

Whole ceps (*Boletus edulis*) are the best dried mushrooms to use in these soups. They can be found in stores selling Middle European foods and the mushrooms are usually strung on strings. They are expensive, but worth the money. They can also be found in supermarkets packed in cellophane bags or in round plastic containers and cut in pieces. The dried Chinese or Japanese *shiitake* (*Lentinus edodes*) mushrooms, the variety most available, may also be used.

MUSHROOM BARLEY SOUP WITH MEAT

10 to 12 servings

The meat may be cut into the soup in small pieces or served separately as boiled beef with a horseradish sauce.

2 oz. dried mushrooms	2 sprigs fresh dill or $1/2$ tsp.
$1/2$ lb. fresh mushrooms	dried dill weed
1 medium onion	4 sprigs parsley
2 lbs. beef	4 celery tops with leaves
beef bones	$1/2$ cup carrots, diced small
$8^1/2$ cups water	$1/2$ cup celery, diced small
$1/2$ cup pearl barley	2 tsp. salt
	$1/8$ tsp. pepper

Soak 2 ounces of dried mushrooms in $1^1/2$ cups of water (see Dried Mushrooms for the amount of time).

Remove the mushrooms from the water and chop them roughly. Line a strainer with a paper towel and pour the mushroom water through it.

Place a chopped onion in the bottom of a large soup pot. Add 2 pounds of beef, some soup bones, and the chopped, soaked mushrooms. Also add the mushroom water and 7 cups more water.

Wash $1/2$ cup pearl barley in warm water and drain. Add it to the pot.

Tie together 4 celery tops with leaves, 2 sprigs of fresh dill, and 4 sprigs of parsley. Lay this bouquet on top and cover. Cook for $1^1/2$ hours.

Remove the tied vegetables and discard. Add $1/2$ cup each of finely diced carrots and celery, 2 teaspoons of salt, and $1/8$ teaspoon of pepper. The soup will be quite thick. (If a thinner soup is desired, add 1 or 2 cups of water.) Cover and cook for 30 minutes more.

Slice $1/2$ pound of mushrooms fine on the large blade of a vegetable grater. Add them to the soup and cook, covered, for 15 more minutes.

Don't wash or peel mushrooms. Wipe clean with fingers, or damp paper towel. Cut a thin slice off the bottom of each stem.

MUSHROOM BARLEY SOUP WITH MILK

10 to 12 servings

For a richer soup, replace some of the milk with cream.

    2 oz. dried mushrooms
 1/2 lb. fresh mushrooms
    2 medium onions, chopped
    5 Tbsp. butter
7 1/2 cups water
    2 tsp. salt
 1/8 tsp. pepper
 1/2 cup pearl barley
    1 quart milk

———————•❦•———————

Soak 2 ounces of dried mushrooms in 1 1/2 cups of water (see Dried Mushrooms for the amount of time).

Remove the mushrooms from the water and chop. Line a strainer with a paper towel and pour the mushroom water through it.

Melt 2 tablespoons of butter in a large soup pot and cook 2 chopped medium onions in it until they are translucent. Add 1 1/2 quarts of water, the mushroom water, the chopped, soaked mushrooms, 2 teaspoons of salt, and 1/8 teaspoon of pepper.

Wash 1/2 cup of pearl barley in warm water and drain. Add it to the pot. Cook covered for 1 1/2 hours.

Slice 1/2 pound of mushrooms fine on the large blade of a vegetable grater. Melt 3 tablespoons of butter in a large skillet, using moderately high heat and when it begins to spatter, sauté the sliced mushrooms for 3 minutes, stirring often.

Add the mushrooms to the soup pot along with 1 quart of milk. Very slowly bring it to a boil.

First Course or Lunch

SCALLOPS IN SHELLS

6 servings

Coquilles Saint-Jacques means scallops in French. On restaurant menus it means scallops with mushrooms served in sauce in a shell.

Mushroom Cheese Sauce (see Index)
1 lb. scallops
2 Tbsp. butter
1 Tbsp. finely chopped shallots or scallions
1/2 cup dry white wine
  grated cheese

———————•◦∞◦•———————

Prepare the recipe for Mushroom Cheese Sauce.

Sea scallops are large and should be sliced or quartered. Bay scallops are small and should be left whole. (If there's a choice, bay scallops are preferred because they are more tender and delicate.) Dry the scallops on paper towels.

In a 1 1/2- or 2-quart saucepan melt 2 tablespoons of butter and add 1 tablespoon of finely chopped shallots or scallions, 1 pound of scallops, and 1/2 cup dry white wine. Simmer the scallops, uncovered for 5 minutes.

Combine the scallops with 1 1/2 cups Mushroom Cheese Sauce (use the extra 1/2 cup over an omelette for breakfast). Spoon this mixture into 6 shells or into baking dishes. Sprinkle with a little grated cheese. Place the filled shells under a broiler, about 4 inches from the heat, and brown.

MUSHROOM QUICHE

Serves 5

Use for a first course, lunch, or light supper.

½ cup Mushroom Duxelles
   (see Index)
   flaky pie pastry for one
      crust shell

2 cups milk or half-and-half
3 eggs
1 Tbsp. flour
½ tsp. salt
⅛ tsp. nutmeg

———————◦⦅⦆◦———————

Line an 8- or 9-inch piepan (or flan ring) with flaky pie pastry. Prick the bottom of the crust well with a fork. Bake for 10 minutes in a 400° oven.

     With a wire whisk, beat together 3 eggs, 1 tablespoon of flour, ½ teaspoon of salt, and ⅛ teaspoon of nutmeg. Add 2 cups of milk or half-and-half (half milk and half cream) and beat again. Add ½ cup or more of Mushroom Duxelles and whip together.

     Pour this mixture into the partially baked pastry shell and bake in a 375° oven for about 30 minutes until the custard is set and the top is brown.

MUSHROOM TARTLETTES

Use the same mixture as for the preceding Mushroom Quiche and fill individual tart shells ¾ full. Enough for about 2 dozen tarts.

Don't wash or peel mushrooms. Wipe clean with fingers, or damp paper towel. Cut a thin slice off the bottom of each stem.

MUSHROOM FRITTERS

12 mushroom fritters

½ lb. mushrooms	1 cup flour
2 eggs	1 tsp. baking powder
½ cup milk	1 tsp. salt
½ medium onion, grated	1 dash cayenne pepper
1 cup oil	

———

Combine 2 eggs with ½ cup of milk in a large bowl. Grate ½ of a medium onion over the egg-milk mixture.

Hook a large strainer over the bowl and sift 1 cup of flour, 1 teaspoon of baking powder, and 1 teaspoon of salt into the bowl. Combine thoroughly to form a smooth batter. Sprinkle with a dash of cayenne pepper.

Slice ½ pound mushrooms thin on the large blade of a vegetable grater. Fold the mushrooms into the batter.

Heat 1 cup of oil in a saucepan to 375° and drop a tablespoon of batter at a time into the hot oil. Brown the fritters on both sides. Serve with sour cream or yogurt for dolloping.

MUSHROOM PIZZA

This mushroom pizza not only has mushrooms on top, but in the dough too. Homemade pizza impresses people more than it should, for it's not difficult. The dough couldn't be easier, being made from the same simple ingredients bread has been made from for centuries: flour, water, leaven, and salt, to which mushrooms are added.

The Mushroom Dough

1/4 lb. mushrooms
1 cup warm water
1 tsp. salt
2 packages dry yeast
3 cups flour

In a cup of warm water sprinkle a teaspoon of salt and 2 packages of yeast. Stir with a spoon until the yeast is thoroughly dissolved. Pour this mixture into a large bowl.

Measure 3 cups of flour (unbleached is best) and sift some over the liquid into the bowl. Stir with a wooden spoon and sift some more, stir, and sift the rest of the flour. When the dough becomes stiff, put down the spoon and use your hands to incorporate all the flour.

Sprinkle a board very lightly with flour and knead the dough with the heels of your hands until it becomes satiny and elastic. Place it in a well-oiled bowl and turn it so that the top is oiled. Cover the bowl with a towel and place it in a warm spot—over a pilot light is good—and let it rise until it has doubled its bulk, about 1 1/2 hours.

Punch the dough down and knead it for a few minutes.

Slice 1/4 pound of mushrooms fine on the large blade of a vegetable grater and chop the slices a little. On a board knead the mushrooms into the dough. This takes only a few minutes.

Divide the dough in half; it will make two pizzas if you use standard pizza pans. A square pan will do, but if you prefer the round look, make two circles of dough and place them each on greased cookie tins.

Pizza dough is not rolled. It is placed on a board and patted into a circle, then it is stretched. It can be stretched by twirling it on your fist, but pulling it into shape will do it too. Be careful not to tear the dough. Shape it into a better circle by tapping it with your fingers. Leave a ridge around the edges. Place the dough on a greased pan.

Don't wash or peel mushrooms. Wipe clean with fingers, or damp
paper towel. Cut a thin slice off the bottom of each stem.

The Mushroom Pizza Sauce

1/4 lb. mushrooms
1 can tomato sauce, 8 oz.
1 can tomato paste, 6 oz.
1/2 tsp. salt
1/4 tsp. basil
1/4 tsp. oregano
1 Tbsp. oil
1/2 lb. mozarella cheese
    grated Parmesan or
        Romano cheese

----------•◦⟨∞⟩◦•----------

In a bowl combine 8 ounces of tomato sauce, 6 ounces of tomato paste, 1/2 teaspoon salt, 1/4 teaspoon each of basil and oregano, and a tablespoon of oil. Mix.

Slice 1/4 pound of mushrooms on the largest blade of a vegetable grater and add them to the sauce. Mix well.

Spread the mushroom sauce on the dough and bake in a preheated 400° oven for 10 minutes.

Shred 1/2 pound of mozarella cheese. Remove the half-baked pizza from the oven and sprinkle with some grated Parmesan or Romano cheese. Top this with the shredded mozarella cheese and return to the oven to bake for 10 minutes more.

ZINGARA MUSHROOMS

4 servings

Zingara mushrooms are one of the delightful inheritances of the Italian Renaissance. They may be served as a vegetable or surround other cooked food. They can also be used as a first course, and they make a fine lunch.

1 lb. small mushrooms	1 small can truffles
1/2 cup Madeira or sherry	(optional)
1 cup flour	3 slices boiled ham
1/2 tsp. salt	4 slices cooked tongue
1/8 tsp. pepper	1/2 tsp. tarragon

Butter a 2-quart casserole well.

In a large bowl pour 1/2 cup Madeira wine or sherry. Add 1 pound of small whole mushrooms and stir to moisten.

Place 1 cup of flour in another bowl (it will not all be used). Remove the moistened mushrooms with a large perforated spoon and drop them, one spoonful at a time, into the bowl containing the flour. Stir the mushrooms to coat them with flour. Remove the mushrooms and shake off any excess flour.

Place them in the buttered casserole. Continue this operation, a spoonful at a time, until all the mushrooms are in the casserole. Sprinkle them with 1/2 teaspoon of salt and 1/8 teaspoon of pepper.

If truffles are used, they should be chopped fine and sprinkled over the mushrooms. Also add the truffle juice.

Cut 3 slices of boiled ham into thin strips and dice 4 slices of cooked tongue. Cover the mushrooms with the meat.

Measure 1/2 teaspoon of dried tarragon into the palm of your hand and crush it between your palms over the casserole. Pour the remaining wine into the casserole, cover, and bake in a 350° oven for 20 minutes.

Don't wash or peel mushrooms. Wipe clean with fingers, or damp paper towel. Cut a thin slice off the bottom of each stem.

MUSHROOMS UNDER GLASS

4 servings

Mushrooms under a glass bell or *champignon sous cloche* give a fine meal that additional touch of elegance which makes one think of the turn of the century, when taste and grace were inseparable parts of fine dining. A first course then was taken more seriously. The cocktail hour (which sometimes lasts for three) wasn't yet invented. Appetites were not dulled with salty potato chips and peanuts, and diners had full appreciation for a delicate dish. Mushrooms under glass is such a dish.

However, as fancy as it is, it can be prepared without the glass bells. Pyrex dishes, carried by most dime stores and hardware stores, will do the job just as well. There are covered pyrex dishes with handles on the sides. These can be inverted, with the covers used as the baking dish. For individual service, the 20-ounce size is best. The mushrooms can also be prepared in a 2-quart covered casserole and spooned out at the table.

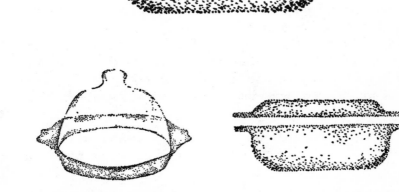

1 lb. mushrooms
4 slices crusty bread
6 Tbsp. butter
1½ Tbsp. lemon juice
½ tsp. dried chervil
½ tsp. salt
⅛ tsp. white pepper
8 Tbsp. heavy cream
4 tsp. sherry

———————•◦‹∞›◦•———————

Cut 4 slices from the wide part of a long loaf of French or Italian bread. Toast them.

In a bowl whip 6 tablespoons of butter for a few minutes until it is fluffy. Whip in 1½ tablespoons of lemon juice, ½ teaspoon of chervil, ½ teaspoon of salt, and ⅛ teaspoon of white pepper. Generously spread the toast with this seasoned butter and place a slice in each of 4 individual baking dishes. If you are using a casserole, line the bottom of it with the buttered toast slices.

Cut the stems from one pound of mushrooms* flush with the underside of the caps. Butter the caps with the seasoned butter. Arrange the caps, round side up, to form a mound of mushrooms on each piece of toast. Pour 2 tablespoons of heavy cream over each of the 4 mushroom mounds.

Cover with glass bells (or pyrex tops or casserole cover) and bake for 25 minutes in a preheated 375° oven. Before serving, lift each bell or cover and pour a teaspoon of sherry over each mound of mushrooms and garnish with a sprig of parsley. Replace the bells or covers and serve.

*It is not essential, but certainly nice, to flute the mushrooms (see Index). If you do, be sure the mushrooms are dried with paper towels before buttering for baking.

Don't wash or peel mushrooms. Wipe clean with fingers, or damp
64 **paper towel. Cut a thin slice off the bottom of each stem.**

MUSHROOM OMELETTES

Methods of preparing omelettes vary from cook to cook. There are those who don't add anything to the eggs, and those who add water, milk, or cream. Some beat the eggs to get air into them, while others stir only enough to combine the yolks with the whites. Some wash the omelette pan, others never do.

Although any number of eggs can be used to make an omelette, the best results are obtained if no more than three are used. It is easier to make a number of small omelettes, rather than cope with one big ungainly one. To be tender, omelettes must be cooked very quickly.

There are many ways to use mushrooms in omelettes. As a general rule, use 2 medium mushrooms for each egg. The mushrooms should be sautéed first in another pan.

Simplest

To make the simplest 2-egg mushroom omelette, slice 4 medium mushrooms fine on the large blade of a vegetable grater and then chop them. Sauté the chopped mushrooms in 1 tablespoon of butter for 3 minutes. Stir them into the eggs and proceed with the omelette.

Enfolded

If the mushrooms are to be enfolded by the omelette, slice the mushrooms fine and sauté them. Add them after the eggs have become firm on the bottom, but while they are still moist on the top. Fold the omelette. Serve immediately.

Fanciest

The fanciest mushroom omelette includes truffles. For a 3-egg omelette use 1 truffle and 12 button mushroom caps. Peel the truffle and chop the peelings very, very fine. Cut a very thin slice from the center of the truffle and reserve for garnish. Chop the rest of the truffle, but not so finely this time. Sauté the chopped truffle with the 12 caps in 1 tablespoon of butter for 4 minutes. Prepare 3 eggs and before folding the omelette add 8 caps and the chopped truffle. Spoon 2 tablespoons of Velvet Mushroom Sauce (see Index) over the omelette and garnish with the slice of truffle in the center and the remaining 4 mushroom caps.

Along with mushrooms, other things can also be added, particularly any one or all of the following herbs: parsley, chives, chervil, and tarragon. If it is an open-faced omelette, not folded, then larger pieces of cooked food can be added, such as fried potatoes, chicken livers, and cubed tomatoes.

Don't forget Mushroom Duxelles—it is a perfect mushroom mixture for omelettes.

Main Dishes

MUSHROOM BURGERS SIMPLE

4 patties

1/2 lb. mushrooms
1/2 lb. chopped beef

————••⟨∞⟩••————

Shred 1/2 pound of mushrooms or slice them fine on the large blade of a vegetable grater. Mix them thoroughly with 1/2 pound of chopped beef. Form into 4 patties. Broil or fry.

MUSHROOM BURGERS FANCY

4 patties

1/2 lb. mushrooms
1/2 lb. chopped beef
 2 Tbsp. dry red wine
 1 egg
   salt and pepper

————••⟨∞⟩••————

Mix 1/2 pound of chopped beef, 2 tablespoons of dry red wine, and an egg together in a bowl. Sprinkle with salt and pepper.
    Shred 1/2 pound of mushrooms or slice them fine on the large blade of a vegetable grater. Add the mushrooms to the meat mixture and shape into 4 patties. Broil or fry. Serve on toasted English muffins.

STUFFED HAMBURGERS SIMPLE

4 stuffed patties

1/4 lb. mushrooms
 1 lb. chopped beef

Divide I pound of chopped beef into 4 equal parts. Divide each quarter in half to make 8 thin patties.

Lay the meat on a large sheet of wax paper and press each patty flat with the palm of your hand. Cup your hands and with the sides of your little fingers and the sides of your palms touching the wax paper, shape the flattened meat into circles.

Slice 1/4 pound of mushrooms fine on the large blade of a vegetable grater. Divide into 4 mounds. Place a mound of mushroom slices on 4 of the patties and cover each with another patty. Work the edges of each patty together with your fingers to form a neatly stuffed hamburger. Then turn it over and pat a little more and the job is even neater. Broil or fry.

Don't wash or peel mushrooms. Wipe clean with fingers, or damp paper towel. Cut a thin slice off the bottom of each stem.

STUFFED HAMBURGERS FANCY

4 stuffed patties

½ lb. mushrooms
1 lb. chopped beef
2 Tbsp. dry red wine
2 oz. blue cheese

————————◄∞►————————

In a bowl soften 1 pound of chopped beef with 2 tablespoons of dry red wine. Slice ½ pound of mushrooms fine on the large blade of a vegetable grater. Mix the mushrooms into the meat thoroughly.

Use half of the mushroom-meat mixture to form 4 large, thin patties.

Crumble 2 ounces of blue cheese and lay about a quarter of it on each patty.

Form 4 more thin patties with the remaining mushroom-meat mixture. Lay them over the blue cheese-topped patties. Work the edges of each patty together with your fingers to form a neatly stuffed hamburger. Turn it over and pat a little more. Broil or fry.

MUSHROOM MEAT BALLS

25 to 30 little meat balls

These meat balls are very light. They can be served as a main dish with a mushroom sauce and flat noodles, are good with spaghetti, and are especially fine as hors d'oeuvres.

1/2 lb. mushrooms	1 tsp. salt
2 shallots or 1 small onion	1/2 tsp. chervil
1/2 lb. chopped beef	1 Tbsp. angostura bitters
1/2 cup bread crumbs	1 Tbsp. chopped parsley
1/4 cup milk	1 egg

Chop fine or grind 1/2 pound mushrooms and 2 shallots or a small onion in a meat grinder using the finest blade. Place the ground mushrooms and shallots or onion in a large bowl and add everything else. Mix thoroughly.

Form into balls about an inch in diameter. Keeping the hands wet helps make the balls more neatly spherical. Roll the balls between your palms and after shaping 5 or 6, rinse your hands under cool water.

Place the meat balls on a flat baking pan. Bake in a preheated 400° oven for 15 minutes.

If you like stronger seasoned meat balls, add 1/2 teaspoon of thyme, and if you're serving them with cocktails use 1/4 cup of dry vermouth instead of the milk.

Don't wash or peel mushrooms. Wipe clean with fingers, or damp paper towel. Cut a thin slice off the bottom of each stem.

ANATOLIAN HAMBURGER

4 servings

1/2 lb. mushrooms	3 Tbsp. chopped parsley
1/2 lb. chopped beef	1 Tbsp. dried mint leaves
1/2 lb. chopped lamb	1 1/2 tsp. salt
3 scallions	1/8 tsp. pepper
1 Tbsp. olive oil	1 Tbsp. lemon juice

1 cup yogurt (1/2 pt.)

———◆◁∞▷◆———

Slice 3 scallions, including most of the green, and sauté in 1 tablespoon of oil in a large skillet over moderately high heat for 2 minutes. Add 1/2 pound each ground beef and lamb. Cook until the pinkness is gone, stirring constantly.

Crush 1 tablespoon of mint leaves between your palms over the skillet and let the mint fall on the meat. Add 3 tablespoons of freshly chopped parsley, 1 1/2 teaspoons of salt, 1/8 teaspoon of pepper, and 1 tablespoon of lemon juice. Mix.

Slice 1/2 pound of mushrooms and add them to the meat. Mix them in well and cook for 5 minutes, using medium heat. Remove from heat and stir in 1/2 pint of yogurt. Serve with bulgur wheat or rice.

MUSHROOM CHILI

4 to 6 servings

1 lb. button mushrooms
1 lb. chopped beef
1 medium onion
1 clove garlic
2 Tbsp. oil
1 lb. can tomatoes
1 to 2 Tbsp. chili powder
1 bay leaf
1 tsp. salt
1 lb. can kidney beans

Chop 1 medium onion and mince 1 clove of garlic. Sauté them in a large skillet in 2 tablespoons of oil over moderately high heat for 2 minutes. Add 1 pound of chopped beef and brown, stirring to prevent lumps.

Add 1 can of tomatoes with its juice, 1 or 2 tablespoons of chili powder (depending upon your taste), 1 bay leaf, and 1 teaspoon of salt. Cover and cook slowly for 1/2 hour.

Add a 1-pound can of kidney beans with its sauce and 1 pound of small button mushrooms. Cover and cook for 10 minutes more.

Don't wash or peel mushrooms. Wipe clean with fingers, or damp
74 *paper towel. Cut a thin slice off the bottom of each stem.*

MUSHROOM MEAT LOAF

4 or 5 servings

This is a fluffy, moist meat loaf. It is more substantial if served with a mushroom sauce. Chilled and sliced thin, it makes a delicious cold cut.

$1/2$ lb. mushrooms	1 egg
$1/2$ lb. ground lean chuck	$1/2$ tsp. basil
2 slices whole-wheat bread	$1/2$ tsp. oregano
1 can (8 oz.) tomato sauce	$1/2$ tsp. chervil
1 small onion	1 tsp. salt

$1/8$ tsp. pepper

Dice 2 slices of bread and place the cubes in a large bowl. Pour 8 ounces of tomato sauce over the cubes and stir.

Grate a small onion over this. Add 1 egg and $1/2$ teaspoon each of basil, oregano, and chervil. Add 1 teaspoon of salt and $1/8$ teaspoon of pepper. Mix well. Add $1/2$ pound of ground chuck and mix again.

Slice $1/2$ pound of mushrooms fine on the large blade of a vegetable grater and mix them into the meat thoroughly.

Bake in a standard meat loaf or bread pan, 9 x 5 x 3, covered with metal foil, in a preheated 350° oven for 50 minutes. Remove foil and continue to bake for 15 minutes longer, when the top will be browned.

PUSHCART POLPETTA

6 servings

In the spring of 1962 the New York City Department of Markets decided the pushcarts selling fresh produce in Greenwich Village were a traffic hazard, old-fashioned, and messy. An order to get rid of them was given. But there was community resistance. A "Save the Pushcarts" Lunch was organized. The following dish was served, and the pushcarts were saved. It's a good buffet dish, especially if you're not sure how many are coming. Serve with spaghetti.

1 lb. mushrooms	1 lb. chopped chuck
1 lb. Italian sweet sausages (6)	1 tsp. salt
	1/2 tsp. oregano
6 Tbsp. oil	1/2 tsp. basil
1 large onion, chopped	2 Tbsp. chopped parsley
1 green pepper, chopped	1 can tomato sauce (8 oz.)
2 stalks celery, chopped	1/4 cup dry red wine

————————•◦❦◦•————————

Remove and chop the stems from 1 pound of mushrooms.

Heat 3 tablespoons of oil in a large skillet over moderately high heat and sauté the mushroom caps, round side down first, for 3 minutes, then turn them over and sauté for 3 minutes more. Remove the caps to a dinner plate and reserve.

In the skillet brown 1 pound of Italian sweet sausages. Remove and reserve. Discard the fat in the skillet and wipe it out with paper towels.

Heat 3 more tablespoons of oil and sauté the chopped mushroom stems, 1 green pepper, 1 large onion, and 2 celery stalks, all cooked until lightly browned. Move them to the side of the skillet and add 1 pound of chopped chuck. Cook until it loses its pink color. Mash it as you mix so it won't lump.

Cut the sausages into 1/2-inch slices and return to the skillet. Add one teaspoon of salt, 1/2 teaspoon each of oregano and basil, 2 tablespoons of fresh chopped parsley, 8 ounces of tomato sauce, and 1/4 cup of dry red wine. Mix. Cover and simmer slowly for 5 minutes. Arrange the mushroom caps on top.

Don't wash or peel mushrooms. Wipe clean with fingers, or damp paper towel. Cut a thin slice off the bottom of each stem.

VEAL KIDNEYS WITH MUSHROOMS

Some dishes, such as veal kidneys, "automatically" call for mushrooms. The following recipe gives the proportions for an individual serving. Multiply for the number of servings required.

This is one of those magnificent dishes that takes only from 5 to 7 minutes to prepare. More cooking would toughen the kidneys and ruin their delicacy. They should be slightly pink inside.

4 medium mushrooms
2 veal kidneys
flour
1½ Tbsp. butter
1 tsp. chopped shallots or
scallions
¼ cup dry wine (red or
white)
1 tsp. chopped parsley

Trim the fat from 2 veal kidneys and peel the thin colorless film surrounding them. Cut the kidneys in 1-inch slices. Roll them in flour and shake off the excess.

Slice 4 medium mushrooms fine on the large blade of a vegetable grater.

In a medium skillet (use a larger size for more servings) heat 1½ tablespoons of butter over moderately high heat. When bubbly, quickly add the kidney slices and shake the pan. After 2 minutes, turn the slices and add a teaspoon of chopped shallots or scallions and the sliced mushrooms. Shake the skillet and stir the mushrooms. Cook 1 minute, then add ¼ cup dry wine and shake the skillet some more.

Sprinkle with salt and freshly ground black pepper and add 1 teaspoon of fresh chopped parsley. Continue to shake the pan. The wine will be greatly reduced and will become the sauce.

FISH FILETS WITH MUSHROOMS

4 servings

This is a naturally fast dish that produces a sauce without even trying.

    1 lb. mushrooms
1½ lbs. fish filets
    flour
    2 Tbsp. butter
    1 Tbsp. oil
    ½ tsp. salt
    pepper
    ½ cup dry white wine
    ⅛ tsp. nutmeg
    1 Tbsp. lemon juice

Separate the stems and caps from 1 pound of mushrooms.

Wipe the filets on paper towels. Dip them in flour and shake off any excess.

In a large skillet heat 2 tablespoons of butter and 1 tablespoon of oil until it begins to spatter. Brown the filets on both sides.

Add the mushrooms, ½ teaspoon of salt, a few turns of the pepper mill, and ½ cup of dry white wine. Cover and simmer for 5 minutes. Sprinkle with ⅛ teaspoon of nutmeg. Add 1 tablespoon of lemon juice and 1 tablespoon of butter and stir them in by tipping the skillet. Spoon the sauce over the fish.

Don't wash or peel mushrooms. Wipe clean with fingers, or damp paper towel. Cut a thin slice off the bottom of each stem.

MUSHROOM GUMBO

4 to 6 servings

To many people gumbo is a soup. In this recipe it becomes a main dish, served with rice.

1 lb. mushrooms	1 clove garlic, minced
1/4 lb. sliced bacon, diced	2 bay leaves, crushed
1 cup raw chicken, cubed	1/2 tsp. thyme
3 slices boiled ham in strips	1/2 tsp. salt
6 scallions, thinly sliced	cayenne
2 cups okra, sliced	black pepper
1 green pepper, diced	2 cups strong chicken broth

2 tsp. gumbo filé

———————◦⊂∞⊃◦———————

Cook 1/4 pound diced bacon in a large skillet over moderately high heat until it begins to brown. Add 1 cup of raw, cubed chicken. Stir until the chicken loses its raw look, about 5 minutes.

Add the following: 3 slices boiled ham cut into thin strips, 2 cups sliced okra, 6 thinly sliced scallions, including some of the green, 1 diced green pepper, 1 minced clove of garlic, 2 crushed bay leaves, 1/2 teaspoon each of thyme and salt, about 10 twists of the pepper mill, a couple of dashes of cayenne pepper, and 2 cups of strong chicken broth. Cover and cook for 10 minutes.

Add 1 pound of whole mushrooms and 2 teaspoons of gumbo filé powder, cover, and cook for 5 minutes more. If you want to make this a more gala dish, add shrimps or oysters or crab meat.

CHICKEN AND MUSHROOMS IN WINE

4 or 5 servings

This dish has a party flavor. It is inexpensive and can be made in advance. The mushroom wine sauce is especially good spooned over rice.

1 lb. mushrooms	1 cup chicken broth
3 to 4 lb. broiler or fryer	$1/2$ cup white wine or dry
1 clove garlic	vermouth
$1/2$ tsp. celery salt	1 tsp. tarragon
$1/8$ tsp. pepper	1 thin slice boiled ham,
2 Tbsp. butter	chopped
1 Tbsp. oil	$1 1/2$ Tbsp. cornstarch
	1 Tbsp. wine

Cut chicken into 8 or more pieces. Rub with a cut clove of garlic. Sprinkle with $1/2$ teaspoon of celery salt and $1/8$ teaspoon of pepper. Broil or roast.

Cut 1 pound of mushrooms into quarters. Heat 2 tablespoons of butter and 1 tablespoon of oil over moderately high heat in a 12-inch skillet until it begins to spatter. Sauté the quartered mushrooms for 3 or 4 minutes. Lower the heat and add the pieces of cooked chicken, 1 cup of chicken broth, $1/2$ cup white wine or dry vermouth, 1 teaspoon of tarragon, and 1 thin slice of boiled ham chopped. Cover and simmer for 5 minutes.

In a small bowl make a paste by combining $1 1/2$ tablespoons of cornstarch with 1 tablespoon of wine. Slowly pour this into the skillet and stir while the sauce thickens. Simmer uncovered for 3 minutes. Taste the sauce for salt and pepper. If a thinner sauce is desired, add a little more chicken broth or wine.

Don't wash or peel mushrooms. Wipe clean with fingers, or damp paper towel. Cut a thin slice off the bottom of each stem.

HAM WITH MUSHROOMS

4 servings

1 lb. mushrooms	2 pimentos (canned)
4 Tbsp. oil	1/4 tsp. tarragon
1 1/2 cups diced cooked ham	1/4 tsp. salt
1 medium onion	1/8 tsp. pepper
2 Tbsp. butter	1 Tbsp. cornstarch
1/2 cup dry sherry	2 Tbsp. chopped fresh
1 Tbsp. dry sherry	parsley
1/2 cup chicken broth	

Cut a pound of mushrooms into quarters.

In a large skillet heat 4 tablespoons of oil and sauté the mushrooms for 3 minutes. Remove them with a perforated spoon.

Sauté 1 1/2 cups diced cooked ham in the same skillet until it is nicely browned. Remove the ham and wipe the skillet with paper towels.

Slice an onion and chop it.

Heat 2 tablespoons of butter until it is bubbly and cook the chopped onion for a few minutes until it begins to take on a golden color. Return the ham and the mushrooms to the pan and add 1/2 cup of dry sherry. Shake the pan and cook for a few minutes, using moderately high heat, until the sherry is reduced to half.

Add 1/2 cup chicken broth. Slice 2 canned pimentos into thin strips and add them to the skillet along with 1/4 teaspoon of tarragon, 1/4 teaspoon of salt, and 1/8 teaspoon of pepper. Cover and simmer for 3 minutes or so.

In a small bowl mix together a tablespoon each of cornstarch and sherry to make a very thin paste. Pour this into the mushrooms and ham and stir until the whiteness disappears and the sauce thickens. Sprinkle the top with 2 tablespoons of fresh chopped parsley. Serve with rice.

SHRIMPS, MUSHROOMS, AND BACON

4 servings

This is a fast, easy basic dish which also lends itself to numerous variations. Any desired combination, or all, of the following may be added: diced green peppers, celery, tomatoes, okra, egg plant, scallops, cubed ham. Herbs and wine add zest. It goes well over rice.

```
 1 lb. mushrooms
 4 slices bacon
 1 small onion, chopped
 1 lb. uncooked shrimp, peeled
1/2 tsp. salt
   pepper
```

Cut 1 pound of mushrooms in quarters.

Chop 4 slices of bacon, not too fine, and fry in a large skillet. When half-cooked, add 1 chopped onion and 2 minutes later add the quartered mushrooms. Stir, and sauté for 3 minutes.

Add 1 pound of uncooked, peeled shrimp and continue stirring. When the shrimp are pink, the dish is done. Sprinkle with 1/2 teaspoon of salt and a few turns of the pepper mill.

PORK CHOPS WITH MUSHROOMS

A sweet-sour taste results from this combination. The recipe gives the method for a single pork chop. Some serve one, some serve 2— it's up to you.

4 mushrooms per chop
1 pork chop
1 apple round
  ground ginger
  salt and pepper
  honey
1 tsp. lemon juice

Cut any excess fat off the pork chop. Brown it on both sides in a skillet.

Sprinkle with ground ginger, salt, and pepper. Place a generous round slice of apple, with skin, on the chop and dribble some honey on the apple. Surround the chop with 4 mushrooms cut in quarters. Add a teaspoon of lemon juice for each chop and cover the pan. Use low heat to steam for 8 to 10 minutes.

VEAL SCALLOPINI WITH MUSHROOMS

4 servings

```
     1 lb. mushrooms
1 1/2 lb. veal scallops
        salt and pepper
        flour
     3 Tbsp. butter
     1 Tbsp. olive oil
     1 Tbsp. shallots or scallions,
        finely chopped
   1/2 cup wine (Marsala, sherry,
        vermouth, or white
        wine)
     1 Tbsp. fresh chopped
        parsley
```

————•◦⦿◦•————

Separate the stems from the caps of 1 pound of mushrooms. Cut each in half.

Flatten the veal scallops. Sprinkle salt and pepper on both sides and dip the pieces lightly in flour. Shake to loosen any excess flour.

In a large skillet heat 3 tablespoons of butter and 1 tablespoon of olive oil over moderately high heat until it begins to spatter but before it browns. Sauté the veal scallops until they are lightly browned on each side, about 5 minutes. Remove them to a platter.

Sauté the mushrooms for 4 minutes in the remaining fat, stirring a few times. Add 1 tablespoon of finely chopped shallots or scallions. Stir and cook for 1 minute more.

Turn the heat down and add 1/2 cup of wine and return the scallops to the skillet. Spoon the mushrooms over the meat. While this is being done the meat and the wine become blended and heated. Sprinkle 1 tablespoon of freshly chopped parsley over it and cook for a minute or two.

84 *Don't wash or peel mushrooms. Wipe clean with fingers, or damp paper towel. Cut a thin slice off the bottom of each stem.*

VEAL CHOPS WITH MUSHROOMS

Follow the preceding recipe except give the chops a few more minutes of cooking time.

LIVER WITH MUSHROOMS

4 servings

1 lb. mushrooms
1½ lb. liver (chicken, calves, beef, or pork)
2 Tbsp. butter
2 Tbsp. oil
2 medium onions, sliced thin

———••◄∞►••———

If chicken livers are used, leave them whole. For other liver, cut into 1-inch strips.

Cut 1 pound of mushrooms in half, including the stems.

Heat 2 tablespoons of butter and one tablespoon of oil in a large skillet over moderately high heat until it begins to spatter. Sauté the mushrooms for 3 or 4 minutes. Remove them to a dinner plate. Do not cover or they will release liquid.

Separate the slices of 2 medium onions into individual rounds. Sauté them in the skillet until they are soft and golden but not browned. Remove the onions to the mushroom plate.

Add another tablespoon of oil and sauté the liver until it begins to brown. Turn and do the same on the other side. Return the mushrooms and onions to the skillet and stir.

MUSHROOM SOUFFLÉ

4 servings

This is my favorite recipe. A special thing happens here—the mushroom slices are suspended throughout the soufflé, which makes it as delicious to eat as it is pretty to look at.

½ lb. mushrooms	1½ cups hot milk
5 Tbsp. butter	¾ cup grated mild cheddar
5 Tbsp. flour	cheese (2 oz.)
1 tsp. salt	6 egg yolks
¼ tsp. paprika	6 egg whites
dash of cayenne	¼ tsp. cream of tartar

Melt 5 tablespoons of butter in a heavy-bottomed saucepan over low heat. Add 5 tablespoons of flour, 1 teaspoon of salt, ¼ teaspoon of paprika, and a dash of cayenne and blend well with a wire whisk.

Pour 1½ cups of hot milk (first ½ cup, then the rest slowly) into the butter-flour mixture. Stir with a wire whisk while the sauce is thickening. Add ¾ cup of grated mild cheddar cheese and continue to stir with the whisk until the cheese is melted. Remove from heat.

Beat 6 yolks into the sauce with the whisk.

Slice ½ pound of mushrooms fine on the large blade of a vegetable grater. Fold the slices into the sauce.

Have 6 egg whites in a large bowl at room temperature. Sprinkle them with ¼ teaspoon cream of tartar. Beat the whites until they are firm but still moist. (If the whites are not firm, they won't be able to sustain the ½ pound of mushroom slices, which will sink to the bottom.)

Pour a couple of spoons of the mushroom sauce lightly over the whites and fold it into them. Continue adding the sauce gently to the white and fold by using an overhand motion. (Overhand,

Don't wash or peel mushrooms. Wipe clean with fingers, or damp paper towel. Cut a thin slice off the bottom of each stem.

away form you; underhand, toward you.) Keep the motion going in the same direction until all the mushroom sauce is incorporated into the whites. Do not stir. The air bubbles formed in the whites must not be broken, as it is precisely the expansion of the hot air in those bubbles which produces the desired puffiness.

Pour the delicate mixture into a well-buttered, 2-quart soufflé dish or casserole and bake in a preheated 350° oven for 45 minutes. It will be gloriously golden and fully blown, rising about 2 inches above the rim of the dish.

BEEF STROGANOFF

4 to 6 servings

Be sure to add the sautéed beef to the Mushrooms in Sour Cream Sauce recipe, not to mushrooms in sour cream. The *sauce* is important.

2 lbs. lean beef
2 Tbsp. butter
1 Tbsp. oil
2 Tbsp. minced onion
   Mushrooms in Sour Cream Sauce recipe (see Index)

Cut 2 pounds of lean beef (it may be tenderloin, sirloin, top round, or chuck) into thin 2-inch strips.

Melt 2 tablespoons of butter and 1 tablespoon of oil in a large skillet. When it begins to spatter, sauté the beef slices as follows: brown on one side, turn over to brown on the other, and add 2 tablespoons of minced onions while the second side is browning.

Combine this meat with Mushrooms in Sour Cream Sauce, the recipe for which will be found in the Vegetable chapter.

MUSHROOM MOUSSE

4 servings as a main course
6 servings as a first course

This is a festive and impressive dish. When it is unmolded onto a large platter and framed with colorful garnishes, it is even more attractive. Serve it in the summer as a main course and in winter as a fabulous first course.

1/2 lb. mushrooms	1 Tbsp. grated onion
1/2 cup water	1 cup diced cooked chicken,
1/4 tsp. salt	cold and tightly packed
1 Tbsp. lemon juice	1 Tbsp. capers
lemon rind	1/8 tsp. nutmeg
1 1/2 cups chicken broth	1 cup heavy cream (1/2 pt.)
1 1/2 Tbsp. unflavored gelatin	
(1 1/2 envelopes)	

In a medium saucepan bring 1/2 cup water, 1/4 teaspoon salt, a tablespoon of lemon juice, and strip of lemon rind to a boil. Cook 1/2 pound of whole mushrooms in this liquid for 5 minutes over moderately high heat, covered. Toss the mushrooms a few times. Remove them with a perforated spoon and spread them out on a large plate to cool. Refrigerate until needed.

Pour 1/2 cup of chicken broth into a medium saucepan. Sprinkle 1 1/2 tablespoons of gelatin on it, to soften. Then heat slowly and stir with a wooden spoon until the gelatin is dissolved. Remove from heat and add a tablespoon of grated onion and 1 more cup of chicken broth. Stir.

Place the chicken broth pot on a bowl full of ice to chill until the broth is syrupy. While the broth is chilling, slice the cooled mushrooms on the large blade of a vegetable grater, then chop them a little. Add the chopped mushrooms to the syrupy broth and stir them in well.

Don't wash or peel mushrooms. Wipe clean with fingers, or damp paper towel. Cut a thin slice off the bottom of each stem.

Arrange the broth pot more firmly on the ice, for some of the ice will have melted. Add a cup of cold, cooked diced chicken, a tablespoon of capers, and $1/8$ teaspoon of nutmeg. Mix thoroughly. Refrigerate while you whip a cup of cold heavy cream with a chilled wire whisk. Place the bowl of cream over the vacated bowl of ice. Beat the cream only until the peaks are soft.

Return the syrupy mushroom-chicken mixture to the ice and fold the whipped cream into it, using an overhand motion. Continue to fold in the cream until the distribution of the chicken and mushrooms is fairly uniform. Turn into a chilled 4-cup mold and refrigerate for at least 3 hours.

FILET OF BEEF WELLINGTON

12 servings

A special party dish which uses mushrooms is Filet of Beef Wellington. It is a whole beef tenderloin, surrounded by chopped mushrooms and wrapped in a crust. This is attractive to look at and sumptuous to eat. A slice of juicy beef is framed with chopped mushrooms and crust.

2 lbs. mushrooms for Mushroom Duxelles (see Index)
  beef tenderloin, 5 or 6 lbs.
  larding fat, sliced thin
  biscuit dough

Follow the directions for Mushroom Duxelles. Two pounds of mushrooms must be cooked in four batches, for if more than $1/2$ pound is cooked at once, the moisture will not be able to evaporate properly.

Remove the fat and skin from a 5- or 6-pound whole tenderloin. Fold the thin end under and tie the beef with a string to create a long, rounded cylindrical shape. Roast the meat for 10 minutes in a preheated 475° oven in a buttered baking pan. Remove to cool.

Prepare the recipe for Mushroom Biscuits, leaving out the mushrooms. The advantage in using biscuit dough is that it is more malleable than pie pastry, making it easier to envelop the filet. To prepare the crust, roll out the dough to 1/2-inch thickness in the shape of a rectangle.

The larding fat may be sheets or strips. (Salt pork is not a substitute, because of the muscular tissue it contains.) Lay the fat between 2 sheets of wax paper and smooth it out with a rolling pin. Line the dough with the fat leaving about a 2-inch border on all sides. Spread duxelles over the fat. Remove the string from the filet. Place the meat on the edge of the duxelles nearest you. Lift the dough and use toothpicks to attach it to the filet while you roll.

When the filet is completely encased, remove the toothpicks and use wet fingers to stick the edges of the dough together, making a smooth-looking wrap. Garnish the top with cut-outs made from the dough. Brush some beaten egg over the whole thing to insure a finished, glossy look.

Allow the meat to "rest" for an hour. Bake it in a preheated 350° oven for 25 minutes on a buttered baking pan. The filet will be rare and the dough will be browned.

MUSHROOM QUENELLES

35 quenelles, 2½ cups shrimp sauce:
6 main course servings

The cultivated mushroom achieves one of its most distinctive refinements in the form of a quenelle. The quenelle is a triumph of classic French cuisine and is generally made of puréed fish or veal or chicken and served in a rich sauce. In texture it is somewhere between a soufflé and a dumpling.

For years I have thought the mushroom could be celebrated in a quenelle despite many obstacles—the quantity of liquid in mushrooms, their inability to absorb cream, and the fact that their color changes after chopping. However, patient experimentation proved that my hunch was right. In the recipe which follows all of the ingredients work to complement the mushroom flavor.

Don't wash or peel mushrooms. Wipe clean with fingers, or damp paper towel. Cut a thin slice off the bottom of each stem.

A mushroom quenelle is essentially rich cream puff dough (*pâté à choux*) with ground mushrooms incorporated into it.

Despite the extraordinary delicacy of this dish, it can be made in advance and refrigerated for a day, or even two. It freezes very well. The quenelles are warmed in the sauce before serving.

The Dough

1 cup flour	1 tsp. salt
2 Tbsp. cornstarch	¾ cup water
¼ lb. sweet butter	4 eggs

Lightly pour 1 cup of flour into a measuring cup. Do not pack it down. Remove 2 level tablespoons of flour and replace them with 2 level tablespoons of cornstarch and stir the starch through the flour.

In a heavy-bottomed, 3- or 4-quart saucepan combine ¼ pound of butter, 1 teaspoon of salt, and ¾ cup of boiling water. Use moderate heat. When the butter has melted, add the cup of cornstarch flour at once. Beat with a wooden spoon for 4 or 5 minutes. A solid yellow mass will be formed.

There should be no flour adhering to the sides of the pot. (This is a vigorous task but it is also an exciting one, for in a matter of minutes a lumpy white liquid becomes transformed into a solid, smooth yellow paste-dough right before your eyes.) Remove from heat.

Beat 4 eggs into the doughlike paste with a wooden spoon, one at a time. The first egg should be thoroughly blended into the mixture before adding the next, and so on.

The Mushrooms

½ lb. mushrooms
2 Tbsp. lemon juice
1 tsp. salt
¼ tsp. nutmeg
⅛ tsp. white pepper

Grind a handful from $1/2$ pound of mushrooms in a meat grinder, using the finest cutting blade. Empty these into the pot containing the dough and sprinkle them with 2 tablespoons of lemon juice, 1 teaspoon of salt, $1/4$ teaspoon nutmeg, and $1/8$ teaspoon of white pepper.

Fold everything into the dough thoroughly. Continue to grind the remaining mushrooms and fold them in. Four grinding and folding operations will be required.

Empty the quenelle mixture into a 3- or 4-quart bowl. Place this bowl in a larger one which contains ice cubes.

Adding the Cream

5 Tbsp. chilled heavy cream

———————•◄∞►••———————

Add 5 tablespoons of cream, 1 tablespoon at a time, to the quenelle paste.

After each spoon of cream is added, blend thoroughly. The quenelle paste bowl remains on ice. The coldness and the beating with the wooden spoon make the mixture firm for the poaching process. If the paste is too soft, the quenelle cannot be properly shaped and will fall apart.

Shaping and Poaching

Each quenelle will be scooped out of the paste-dough, shaped, and poached, uncovered, in the skillet. You will need 2 spoons (large dessert or small soup) and a cup of hot water.

Butter a 12-inch skillet well. Place it next to the bowl of mushroom quenelle paste on the work table. Scoop out an oval mass of paste with the scooping spoon. Wet the shaping spoon in the cup of hot water; remove it and smooth the top of the oval mass of paste. This is done by placing the wet inverted spoon over the mass of quenelle paste.

Don't wash or peel mushrooms. Wipe clean with fingers, or damp paper towel. Cut a thin slice off the bottom of each stem.

Slide the quenelle off the scooping spoon, on its side, into the skillet by slipping the wet shaping spoon under it. Return the shaping spoon to the cup of water. Scoop out another quenelle and smooth the top with the inverted shaping spoon. Slide the quenelle into the skillet and repeat until the skillet is full. This will use about

$1/2$ of the mixture and will make about 17 quenelles. They should be placed as close to each other as possible without touching.

Place the skillet on the stove and carefully, from the side, pour from 1 to 2 inches of very hot water into it. The quenelles will float. Sprinkle a couple of teaspoons of salt into the water. Use very low heat; the poaching water must remain just under a simmer. Boiling water will split the quenelles. Turn them over after about 10 minutes of poaching and continue for from 5 to 10 minutes more until they are firm. Remove the quenelles with a perforated spoon to a dish towel or paper towels for draining.

Wash the skillet and rinse with cold water before drying. Butter the skillet. Repeat the process again to use up the rest of the quenelle paste. If they are to be refrigerated or frozen, they should be buttered individually after they have drained and are cooled. This is simply done with your fingers. Use butter which has been sitting at room temperature and is very soft. Place the quenelles in an airtight plastic container.

SHRIMP SAUCE FOR QUENELLES

2½ cups shrimp sauce for 35 quenelles

Shrimp

½ lb. shrimp
1½ cups water
1 bay leaf
1 tsp. salt
2 celery stalks with leaves
1 small onion, sliced
3 sprigs parsley
8 peppercorns
1 Tbsp. lemon juice

Cook everything except the shrimp for 10 minutes, covered. Add the shrimp and cook them uncovered for 3 or 4 minutes until they become pink. Remove the shrimp from the resulting court bouillon with a perforated spoon and peel under cold running water. Slice them into ½-inch pieces. Strain the court bouillon.

Don't wash or peel mushrooms. Wipe clean with fingers, or damp paper towel. Cut a thin slice off the bottom of each stem.

Sauce

4 Tbsp. butter
5 Tbsp. flour
1 cup hot court bouillon
1 cup milk

1/4 cup dry white wine
5 Tbsp. heavy cream
1/2 lb. shrimp (preceding recipe)

1 Tbsp. lemon juice

In a large skillet melt 4 tablespoons of butter over low heat. (The heat is low throughout this recipe.) Cream 5 tablespoons of flour with it, using a wire whisk. Cook for 2 minutes, stirring all the time. Add 1 cup of hot court bouillon (which shrimp from the preceding recipe were cooked in)—first 1/2 cup, then the rest slowly. Beat with whisk. Add 1 cup of milk slowly, stirring all the time. Cook sauce for 3 minutes.

Add 1/4 cup dry white wine, 5 tablespoons of heavy cream, and 1/2 pound of sliced shrimp. Stir. Taste for salt and pepper. Add 1 tablespoon of lemon juice. Stir. Place the quenelles in the sauce and carefully spoon sauce over each one. Cover and let them steam to heat for 5 minutes.

Mushroom quenelles are best served at the table from a chafing dish or a heated covered casserole. As a main dish, serve 5 per person. As a first course, serve 2 or 3.

This distinguished *oeuvre* should be served with a chilled white wine which is soft and graceful, rather than full-bodied. The fruity, fragrant Pouilly-Fumé is ideal.

MUSHROOM ROAST

6 servings

This is a completely vegetarian dish. It has the substantial quality of a roast, without containing meat. It is best served with a mushroom sauce.*

1½ lbs. mushrooms	½ cup bread crumbs
2 large potatoes	1 tsp. baking powder
3 large carrots	½ tsp. marjoram
1 medium onion	½ tsp. savory
2 stalks celery	1½ tsp. salt
3 Tbsp. chopped parsley	¼ tsp. pepper
2 eggs	2 Tbsp. oil

1 Tbsp. lemon juice

———————•·•◁∞▷•·•·—————————

Grate 2 potatoes, 3 carrots and an onion into a large bowl.

Chop 2 celery stalks into medium dice and add them, along with 3 tablespoons of freshly chopped parsley and 2 eggs. Mix well.

To ½ cup bread crumbs add a teaspoon of baking powder, ½ teaspoon each of marjoram and savory, 1½ teaspoons of salt, and ¼ teaspoon of pepper. Stir these dry ingredients, then sprinkle them over the grated vegetables.

Add 2 tablespoons of oil and a tablespoon of lemon juice and blend it all together.

Coarsely chop 1½ pounds of mushrooms, a handful at a time, and add them to the vegetable mixture as you chop. By stirring them into the body of the roast you protect their color. Mix well.

Pour into a well-greased, 2-quart casserole and bake in a pre-heated 350° oven for 1 hour covered. Uncover and bake for 15 minutes longer to nicely brown the roast.

*Use Basic Mushroom Sauce I (see Index) and substitute small whole button mushrooms for the sliced ones.

Mushrooms as a Vegetable,
and with Vegetables

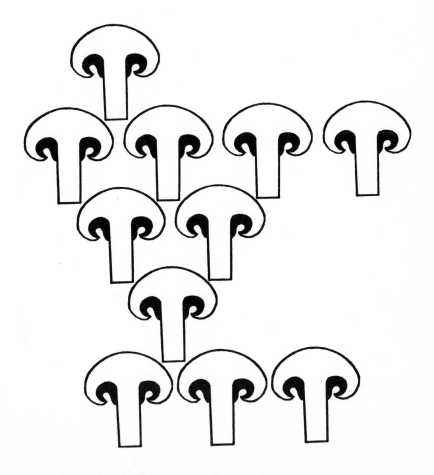

MUSHROOMS IN SOUR CREAM

Serves 4

An exotic vegetable to serve which couldn't be easier to make.

1 lb. mushrooms
3 Tbsp. butter
1 cup sour cream (½ pt.)
  salt and pepper
  fresh chopped parsley

Use 1 pound of button mushrooms or halve larger ones. Sauté them in 3 tablespoons of bubbly butter in a large skillet over moderately high heat for 3 minutes. Stir often.

Remove from heat and stir in 1 cup sour cream, which is at room temperature. Sprinkle with salt and pepper and serve garnished with freshly chopped parsley.

MUSHROOMS ALMONDINE

4 servings

Serve this as a special vegetable. The contrast in textures is delightful.

Use 1 pound of mushrooms. Follow the directions for sautéed mushrooms. After sautéeing, move them to the side of the skillet and add another tablespoon of butter. Lightly brown 2 tablespoons of thinly sliced blanched almonds in the butter. This will take about 1 minute. The almonds should be carefully watched and stirred, for they can burn very quickly. Mix the mushrooms and the almonds together.

SAUTÉED MUSHROOMS

4 servings

Sautéeing is the most common method of preparing mushrooms. To sauté correctly means to fry in a small quantity of very hot fat in an open skillet, thus sealing in the juices and browning the mushrooms. The mushrooms must be dry. If they are damp or too closely packed in the skillet, they will steam instead of sauté. A layer of steam will develop between them and the fat, preventing the searing process.

A pound of large mushrooms can be sautéed at one time in a 12-inch skillet. The stems should be separated from the caps to allow the heat to penetrate the caps more easily. If you are using the caps solely as a garnish, use the stems for a soup or a sauce. Otherwise sauté the stems too, at the same time. If the mushrooms are small, the stems may be left on. But they should be sautéed in two batches, using half the amount of fat each time. To sauté slices, more fat is needed.

1 lb. mushrooms
2 Tbsp. butter
1 Tbsp. oil
  salt and pepper

Remove the stems from 1 pound of mushrooms. Heat 2 tablespoons of butter and 1 tablespoon of oil over moderately high heat until it is bubbly and starts to spat. Although the fat must be very hot, it must not brown.

Place the mushroom caps in the skillet, round side down, then add the stems. The mushrooms will absorb the fat almost immediately, but don't add any more, just shake the skillet. Mushrooms have a specific point of absorption. Additional fat will only remain in the pan, serving no positive function. After 2 minutes turn the

Don't wash or peel mushrooms. Wipe clean with fingers, or damp paper towel. Cut a thin slice off the bottom of each stem.

caps over and shake the skillet from time to time. Sauté for 2 more minutes.

Sprinkle with salt and pepper before serving. If the mushrooms must wait for other food, be certain not to cover them. A cover will cause a change in texture and the mushrooms will release their juice. If you want to warm them again, heat for a minute.

FLAMING MUSHROOMS

4 servings

This is a flamboyant dish. A fuss should be made about it—it's that kind of thing. The chafing dish is perfect for the finish but the sautéeing should be done in the kitchen. The cooking ritual at the table must be quick and dramatic, otherwise it can become a bore. And who wants that!

½ lb. mushrooms	2 Tbsp. brandy
3 Tbsp. butter	4 Tbsp. heavy cream
½ cup sherry	salt

Use ½ pound of small to medium mushrooms. Leave the stems on. Sauté them in 3 tablespoons of butter over moderately high heat. After they have begun to brown, add ¼ cup of sherry. Shake the skillet. When the sherry has boiled down a little, add another ¼ cup. Continue cooking until the sherry is reduced and syrupy. This will take less than 5 minutes. Transfer the mushrooms to a chafing dish, using a rubber scraper. Be sure the chafing dish has its water boiling and the burner lit.

When you are ready to serve the mushrooms, pour 2 tablespoons of brandy over them and ignite. When the flame burns out, add 4 tablespoons of heavy cream. Sprinkle with a little salt and stir. Be sure you have crusty bread at the meal for this sauce is for wiping up. A broiled steak couldn't find a better complement.

MUSHROOM PURÉE

6 servings

The classic recipe for mushroom purée requires squeezing the juice out in cheesecloth. This means loss of flavor; therefore the recipe given here eliminates that step.

Mushroom purée is a very rich and delicate vegetable which goes well with baked or broiled fish or poultry, or with roast veal. It is usually served in individual bowls, but when it is spooned onto the same plate with the fish or meat, it acts as a sauce too. A spoon or two over plain rice makes the rice luxurious.

This is one of those dishes one must play with. That is, it really can't be prepared with any pressure around, such as cocktail drinkers keeping the cook company. It demands the cook's total attention, for it must be coaxed along, not rushed. It isn't difficult, it's just that there are built-in hazards, such as lemon juice with heavy cream, mushrooms darkening, and moisture to get rid of *slowly*. It's worth the trouble and can be prepared in advance.

1 lb. mushrooms	1/2 tsp. salt
5 Tbsp. butter	white pepper
3 Tbsp. flour	1 Tbsp. lemon juice
1 cup heavy cream (1/2 pt.)	nutmeg

Over low heat, in a 1- or 2-quart saucepan melt 2 tablespoons of butter and mix 3 tablespoons of flour with it until smooth, using a wire whisk. Very slowly, pour 1 cup of heavy cream into the flour-butter mixture, stirring all the time with the whisk. Allow it gradually to come to a boil and simmer for 3 minutes as the sauce

Don't wash or peel mushrooms. Wipe clean with fingers, or damp paper towel. Cut a thin slice off the bottom of each stem.

thickens, stirring with the whisk all the time. Add $\frac{1}{2}$ teaspoon of salt and a few sprinkles of white pepper. Turn the heat off.

Pour 1 tablespoon of lemon juice into an electric blender. Cut $\frac{3}{4}$ of a pound of mushrooms into quarters, or smaller pieces if the mushrooms are large. Using high speed throughout, blend some mushroom pieces with the lemon juice. Pour some of the sauce from the stove into the blender and turn it on and off. Blend the mushrooms and the sauce interchangeably until both are used. This is like making blender mayonnaise, for toward the end the mushroom pieces remain on top and have to be coaxed into the purée. When this happens, turn the machine off and start again. If the pieces of mushroom persist in remaining on top of the purée instead of getting into it, then, with the blender turned off, spoon some purée over the pieces, replace the cover, and continue.

Slice the remaining $\frac{1}{4}$ of a pound of mushrooms on the largest blade of a vegetable grater and chop them a little. Melt 3 tablespoons of butter in a large saucepan and when it is bubbly add the chopped mushrooms. Cook them for about 4 minutes, stirring all the time with a wooden spoon. This will separate the pieces and permit steam to escape. The chopped mushrooms should not brown. Turn the heat off and add the purée from the blender. Use a rubber scraper to get all the purée out.

Using the *lowest* heat possible, cook the purée. Stir continuously with the wooden spoon. The purée will steam and thicken as it cooks. It is extremely important to keep the heat low, because this step cannot be rushed; the purée must *not* boil. After about 6 minutes of this close stirring, the purée will coat the spoon. Add a couple of dashes of nutmeg and stir. Remove from the heat and let it cool. When the pot is cool enough to refrigerate, float a little cream or milk on top to prevent the formation of a hard, dark skin. Heat very slowly before serving.

MUSHROOMS IN CREAM

The classic method does not use the stems. But if you want to, sauté them with the caps.

4 servings

1 lb. mushrooms
4 Tbsp. butter (1/2 stick)
2 Tbsp. flour

1 cup light cream (1/2 pt.)
1/2 tsp. salt
white pepper
1/2 tsp. lemon juice

In a small saucepan melt one tablespoon of butter over low heat and blend 2 tablespoons of flour with it, using a wire whisk. Add a cup of light cream and let it come to a boil, stirring with the whisk all the time. Remove from heat.

Remove the stems from a pound of mushrooms. Sauté the caps, round side down, in a large skillet in 3 tablespoons of bubbly butter, using moderately high heat for about 3 minutes until they are brown. Turn the caps over and lower the heat.

Pour the cream sauce over the mushroom caps, cover the skillet, and simmer gently for 5 minutes. Remove from the heat and add 1/2 teaspoon of salt, a couple of dashes of white pepper, and 1/2 teaspoon of lemon juice. Stir. Serve on toast or in patty shells.

Don't wash or peel mushrooms. Wipe clean with fingers, or damp paper towel. Cut a thin slice off the bottom of each stem.

BROILED MUSHROOMS

Broiled mushrooms usually means only the caps. Serve them on buttered toast, or as hors d'oeuvres or a garnish.

large mushrooms
butter or oil
salt
pepper

Remove the stem from each mushroom by snapping it to one side.

If you prefer butter, make sure it is very soft from sitting at room temperature. With your fingers butter each cap well on both sides.

If you prefer oil, olive or any other, pour some into a small bowl and with your fingers wipe oil over each cap, including the underside.

Arrange the caps, round side up, and place them in a shallow pan under a preheated broiler about 5 inches from the heating unit. Broil for 4 or 5 minutes, then turn them and broil for 4 or 5 minutes more. Sprinkle with salt and pepper.

STEWED MUSHROOMS

Stewed mushrooms are versatile. They can be served buttered as a vegetable, used as a garnish, or can be added to enrich other dishes at the last minute. The lemon juice helps to keep them white. They can be kept in the refrigerator for four days. Use their cooking liquid in a sauce, or reduce it by boiling and freeze the essence for later use.

1 lb. mushrooms
$1/2$ cup water
$1/2$ tsp. salt
2 Tbsp. lemon juice

Bring $1/2$ cup of water, $1/2$ teaspoon of salt, and 2 tablespoons of lemon juice to a boil in a 2- or 3-quart saucepan. Add I pound of whole mushrooms and cover. Boil over moderate heat for 5 minutes, tossing them a few times.

The mushrooms should remain in their liquid until ready for use. If you wish to store, leave in liquid and place in a tightly covered container in the refrigerator.

Don't wash or peel mushrooms. Wipe clean with fingers, or damp paper towel. Cut a thin slice off the bottom of each stem.

MUSHROOMS IN SOUR CREAM SAUCE

4 servings

The tartness provided by the sour cream is especially pleasant when this vegetable is served with a roast or broiled food. Combined with browned beef, this makes Beef Stroganoff.

1 lb. button mushrooms or larger ones cut in half
1 cup chicken broth
1 Tbsp. butter
1 Tbsp. flour
1 cup sour cream (¹/₂ pt.)

Boil 1 pound of button mushrooms in 1 cup of chicken broth for 5 minutes, covered.

In a small saucepan, over low heat, melt 1 tablespoon of butter and cream 1 tablespoon of flour with it. Stir for a couple of minutes with a wire whisk. Pour some of the hot broth into the butter-flour mixture and beat. Add the rest of the broth without the mushrooms and continue to beat.

Pour this sauce over the mushrooms and let it slowly come to a boil. Simmer for a few minutes. Remove from heat and stir in 1 cup of sour cream, at room temperature. Taste for salt and pepper.

MUSHROOMS À LA BORDELAISE

4 servings as vegetable

A la Bordelaise, with mushrooms, always means sautéed with shallots and tossed with bread crumbs. Traditionally this dish is listed as *Cepes à la Bordelaise.* However, the recipe applies equally to cultivated mushrooms as well as the wild ceps. Incidentally, a one-pound can of ceps ranges from 89¢, if you're very lucky, to over $2. Or pick them yourself. See the chapter on Wild Mushrooms where the cep is described.

Served as a vegetable, these are noteworthy; with dry vermouth before dinner, they're outstanding; as a garnish, remarkable.

1 lb. mushrooms or	2 Tbsp. chopped shallots or
1 lb. can of ceps*	scallions
2 Tbsp. butter	1 small clove garlic (optional)
1 Tbsp. olive oil	2 Tbsp. bread crumbs
	salt and pepper

Remove the stems from the mushrooms.

Heat 2 tablespoons of butter and 1 tablespoon of oil in a large skillet until it is bubbly. Sauté the mushroom caps 2 or 3 minutes on each side to brown them.

Add 2 tablespoons of finely chopped shallots or the whites of scallions with a small clove of garlic, finely minced, and 2 tablespoons of bread crumbs. Shake the skillet to combine all the ingredients and turn the mushrooms so that the crumb mixture adheres to them. Continue to shake the skillet for about 3 minutes. Sprinkle with salt and pepper.

*If you are using a can of ceps, pour them into a strainer and save the liquid they were packed in for a sauce. If the mushrooms are small, leave them whole; if they are large, remove the stems and slice them in small pieces, for they need more cooking than the caps. Dry them well on paper towels before sautéeing and proceed with the recipe except give the ceps a few more minutes cooking before adding the shallots and crumbs.

Don't wash or peel mushrooms. Wipe clean with fingers, or damp paper towel. Cut a thin slice off the bottom of each stem.

BEAN SPROUTS WITH MUSHROOMS

4 to 6 servings as a vegetable

Bean sprouts are a marvelous vegetable and come as a surprise when served with anything but a Chinese meal. They're inexpensive, nutritious, and make a wonderful change.

1/2 lb. mushrooms
1 lb. can bean sprouts
3 Tbsp. oil
1 medium onion
1 cup chicken broth
1 Tbsp. cornstarch
1 Tbsp. soy sauce

Open a 1-pound can of bean sprouts and drain them in a strainer. Cut a medium onion into thin slices and separate the rings. Slice 1/2 pound of mushrooms on the large blade of a vegetable grater.

In a large skillet heat 3 tablespoons of oil using moderately high heat and cook the onion rings for about 2 minutes, stirring them so they don't brown. Add the mushroom slices and continue to stir for 3 or 4 minutes.

Add the bean sprouts and stir. Add a cup of chicken broth and stir some more. While this is cooking, mix together in a small bowl a tablespoon each of cornstarch and soy sauce to make a thin paste. Add the paste to the skillet and stir until the sauce thickens, a couple of minutes.

This dish lends itself to expansions, such as the addition of garlic, ginger, a little sherry, and a slice of boiled chopped ham. Any or all of these could be included. This recipe also can be used as the basis of a main dish by adding chicken, fish, shellfish, or meat. You would then want more sauce, so double the amount of cornstarch and add another 1/2 cup of broth.

DRIED LIMAS WITH DRIED MUSHROOMS

6 servings

Overnight soaking is a very important step in this recipe. It not only expands the beans and mushrooms, but provides the natural liquid the dish is to be cooked in.

2 to 6 oz. dried wild mushrooms	4 cloves
1 lb. dried baby lima beans	1 bay leaf
large ham bone or 4 smoked ham hocks	2 Tbsp. brown sugar
1 onion	celery tops
	2 cloves garlic
	2 tsp. salt

¼ tsp. pepper

Wash 1 pound of dried baby lima beans. Place them in a pot and pour 2 quarts of water over them. If any beans rise to the top, discard them. Add 2 to 6 ounces dried wild mushrooms (2 ounces are good, 6 ounces are superlative). If they are whole, break them into pieces. Soak uncovered overnight.

When you are ready to cook the beans, add a large meaty ham bone or 4 smoked ham hocks to the pot. Stick 4 cloves into a peeled onion and add it to the bean pot along with a bay leaf, 2 tablespoons of brown sugar, 4 or 5 celery tops with lots of green leaves tied together with string, 2 cloves of garlic, minced, 2 teaspoons of salt, and ¼ teaspoon of pepper. Cook the beans in the same water they soaked in. Bring to a boil, turn the heat down low, and cover. Simmer for 1½ hours.

Remove the celery, onion, and bay leaf and discard. If you like the beans softer, cook them some more. If you want less liquid, cook them uncovered, using high heat until the juice is reduced. As a variation, add ½ pound of fresh, sliced sautéed mushrooms just before serving. The dried and the fresh mushrooms together make a wonderful combination.

Don't wash or peel mushrooms. Wipe clean with fingers, or damp paper towel. Cut a thin slice off the bottom of each stem.

MUSHROOM SOLIANKA

8 servings

This is an adaptation of a classic Russian dish. But as with all classics, every province has its variation. Cabbage, cucumbers, and mushrooms are the basics, and they always remain. Dried mushrooms are sometimes added and they, of course, enhance the dish. They should be broken into pieces and soaked for 2 hours, then chopped and mixed through the cabbage.

1 lb. mushrooms	1 can tomato sauce, 8 oz.
small head cabbage, 1 to 1½ lbs.	2 tsp. sugar
2 Tbsp. butter	1 tsp. salt
1 Tbsp. vinegar	⅛ tsp. pepper
1 onion, medium-to-small	2 cucumbers
	bread crumbs
butter	

Wash the cabbage and slice into thin strips. Place it in a 4-quart saucepan and add ½ cup of water, 2 tablespoons of butter, and 1 tablespoon of vinegar. Cover and cook for 5 minutes. Turn the heat off and let the cabbage rest for a few minutes, still covered.

Grate an onion on top of the cabbage and add an 8-ounce can of tomato sauce, 2 teaspoons of sugar, 1 teaspoon of salt, and ⅛ teaspoon of pepper. Mix well.

Butter a 2-quart casserole and place half of the cabbage mixture in it.

Peel 2 cucumbers. Quarter and dice them. Lay them on the cabbage. Cut 1 pound of mushrooms in thick slices and lay them on the cucumbers. Add the remaining half of the cabbage and sprinkle with bread crumbs. Dot the top with butter.

Bake uncovered in a preheated 375° oven for 25 minutes.

GREENS

Greens with mushrooms are the Ying and Yang of vegetable gastronomy. One is loaded with chlorophyll and the other is totally devoid of it. Cook your favorite greens the way you like them and add mushrooms to the pot for the last 5 minutes of covered cooking time. A 10-ounce package of frozen greens can be substituted for a pound of fresh ones in the following recipes.

SPINACH

4 or 5 servings

1/2 lb. button mushrooms
 1 lb. spinach
 2 Tbsp. olive oil
 2 Tbsp. chopped onion

1 Tbsp. lemon juice
1/2 tsp. salt
1/4 tsp. nutmeg
 pepper

Remove the coarse stems from the spinach. Wash well to remove all the sand. Drain.

In a large, heavy-bottomed saucepan (avoid aluminum or iron for the spinach will take on a metallic taste) heat 2 tablespoons of olive oil over moderately high heat.

Sauté 2 tablespoons of chopped onion with 1/2 pound of button mushrooms for 2 or 3 minutes.

Add the spinach and 1 tablespoon of lemon juice, 1/2 teaspoon of salt, 1/4 teaspoon of nutmeg, and a few turns of the pepper mill. Stir and move the bottom leaves to the top. Cover. Cook for 3 minutes. If you like your spinach wilted more, merely leave it in the pot with the cover on, but the heat turned off. The steam and the heat of the pot will cook it further.

Don't wash or peel mushrooms. Wipe clean with fingers, or damp paper towel. Cut a thin slice off the bottom of each stem.

MUSTARD GREENS

6 servings

There are many varieties of mustard greens. They range from large leafy stalks to what appears to be baby broccoli spears, with tiny yellow flowers on the clusters and hardly any leaves at all. There are about 10 different kinds, all good, and all are cooked the same way, for not more than 10 minutes.

$\frac{1}{2}$ lb. mushrooms
 1 lb. mustard greens
 2 Tbsp. butter
 2 Tbsp. minced shallots or
     whites of scallions
$\frac{1}{2}$ tsp. salt
 1 hard-cooked egg
     paprika

--------•◀◇▶•--------

Wash the mustard greens and drain.

In a 3- or 4-quart saucepan melt 2 tablespoons of butter and sauté 2 tablespoons of minced shallots or scallions for 1 minute.

Add the mustard greens and pour in some boiling water to cover the bottom of the pan, about 4 tablespoons. Cover and cook for 5 minutes over moderate heat.

Slice $\frac{1}{2}$ pound of mushrooms and add them to the mustard greens along with $\frac{1}{2}$ teaspoon of salt. Cover and cook for 5 minutes.

Serve garnished with hard-cooked egg slices. Sprinkle some paprika on the yolks.

COLLARD GREENS

4 servings

Collards are the greens usually referred to when pot liquor is mentioned. That taste, which is very good, is quite different from the recipe given here. Those are cooked long, these are not, and have a crispiness.

If frozen collards are used, ignore the cooking directions on the package and merely substitute them in this recipe for the fresh ones. No more water than the amount that adheres to the leaves is necessary.

1/2 lb. mushrooms
1 lb. collard greens
3 strips bacon
1/2 tsp. salt
pepper

Wash the collard greens by holding them under cold running water. Cut the stems off. If the stems are tough and run deep into the leaves, strip them out.

Slice the leaves across in 1 1/2- or 2-inch widths.

Dice 3 strips of bacon and render in a large saucepan. Add the cut collards, stir, and cover. Cook for 4 minutes, using moderate heat.

Cut 1/2 pound of mushrooms in quarters and add them to the collards with 1/2 teaspoon of salt and a few twists of a pepper mill. Cover and cook for 5 minutes. This gives a crispy, chewy green, very different from the others.

Don't wash or peel mushrooms. Wipe clean with fingers, or damp paper towel. Cut a thin slice off the bottom of each stem.

DANDELION GREENS

4 to 6 servings

Dandelion greens have for centuries, among many diverse cultures, been used as a healthful spring tonic, especially to supply vigor.

The U.S. Department of Agriculture handbook *Composition of Foods* tells us 1 cup of cooked dandelion greens contains 27,310 units of vitamin A, 337 milligrams of calcium, 126 milligrams of phosphorus, and many more impressive nutrients. With all of that, they taste marvelous too. Dandelion greens have a bitterness similar to that of vermouth, sweet or dry. If you live in a large city, you can get them throughout most of the year in Italian neighborhoods. Vitamins and vigor aside, the dandelion greens with mushrooms are a distinguished vegetable, particularly when served with plain broiled meat.

½ lb. mushrooms
1 lb. dandelion greens
1 Tbsp. olive oil
1 clove garlic

Wash the dandelion greens and trim the stems. Do not cut the leaves, merely twist them around your fork to eat. Drain in a salad basket or colander.

Mince a clove of garlic. Cut the mushrooms in quarters. In a 3-quart saucepan heat a tablespoon of oil and, for 1 minute only, brown the garlic. Quickly add the greens and mushrooms and cover. The amount of water that adheres to the leaves is all that is necessary. Cook for 5 minutes over moderate heat. Stir once during that time. The mushrooms and greens release juices which make a fine sauce. These greens become reduced very much when cooked.

POTATOES

Mushrooms do for potatoes what wine does for stew. They not only bring out the potato flavor, they enhance it. Mushrooms may be added to all potato dishes. Some outstanding ones are given below.

MASHED POTATOES WITH MUSHROOMS

6 servings

Mashed potatoes can be delectable if they are light and fluffy. It is very important to "dry them out" after draining and before mashing. Baking powder helps expand them (which is necessary in order to absorb the quantity of milk needed to make them extra fluffy). The mushroom slices are suspended throughout.

½ lb. mushrooms	¾ cup milk
4 large potatoes	½ medium onion, grated
3 Tbsp. butter	1 tsp. baking powder
1 tsp. salt	

Peel 4 large potatoes. Quarter, and cut each quarter in half. Boil in a 3-quart saucepan with enough water to cover until the potatoes are tender, about 30 minutes. Drain them of all their cooking water and return to the stove. Shake the pan over moderate heat for a few minutes to "dry out" the potatoes.

While the potatoes are boiling, slice ½ pound of mushrooms on the largest blade of a vegetable grater. Sauté them in a large skillet in 3 tablespoons of butter for about 3 or 4 minutes. Let them remain in the open skillet until they are needed. Do not cover or they will release moisture.

After drying the potatoes, turn the heat down as low as possible and add ½ cup of milk. While the milk is heating, add 1 tea-

116 *Don't wash or peel mushrooms. Wipe clean with fingers, or damp paper towel. Cut a thin slice off the bottom of each stem.*

spoon of baking powder, 1 teaspoon of salt, $\frac{1}{8}$ teaspoon of white pepper, and $\frac{1}{2}$ medium onion, grated.

Mash the potatoes with a masher or an electric hand mixer. Add $\frac{1}{4}$ cup more milk and whip the potatoes. Add the sautéed mushrooms and fold them in well. Cover the pot and allow the potatoes to steam for a few minutes. They'll get even fluffier. Dot each serving with butter.

PRINCESS POTATOES

Add a beaten egg to the preceding recipe for Mashed Potatoes with Mushrooms and blend it in well.

Butter a baking sheet and neatly spoon out mounds of potatoes. Shape them with the back of a spoon. Put a generous dot of butter on the top of each mound and bake in a hot preheated 450° oven for about 7 minutes. The potato mounds will be firm enough to lift off individually and will be nicely browned and buttery.

QUEEN POTATOES

Potatoes fit for a queen, or a king too. These are very fancy mashed potatoes with mushrooms, piped through a pastry bag and garnished with a sautéed button mushroom cap.

For Queen Potatoes, follow the directions for Mashed Potatoes with Mushrooms, but after slicing the mushrooms, chop them fine, too. This is necessary to insure an easy flow through the pastry-bag tube. After adding the chopped sautéed mushrooms to the potatoes, add a beaten egg and mix it in well.

Use a plastic-lined bag for piping the potatoes, not a cloth one or the milk will become absorbed by the cloth and lightness will be lost. The prettiest mounds are made by using a many-pointed tube (Ateco 6B is perfect).

Butter a baking sheet and form the potato-mushroom mound by piping a circle on the pan and continue forming smaller circles as you build up to a point. Dot with butter and garnish with a sautéed button mushroom cap. Bake in a hot preheated 450° oven for about 7 minutes. These mushroom-potatoes make one of the most attractive garnishes surrounding other cooked food, particularly a rib roast or a steak.

POTATO MUSHROOM PANCAKES

About 15 pancakes

If a recipe could be called diet-dangerous, this one is. These pancakes are so tempting that most cooks can't resist eating three or four from the first batch while they are draining. Yes, they're fattening but the taste is worth the calories. Try them. If you find that you're an undisciplined sampler, switch to the recipe for Potato Mushroom Pudding next time.

1/2 lb. mushrooms	1/8 tsp. white pepper
4 medium potatoes	2 Tbsp. flour
1 onion, medium to small	1 tsp. cornstarch
1 egg	1 tsp. baking powder
1 tsp. salt	oil for frying

———————•◄∞►•·————————

Peel 4 medium potatoes. Dice them one at a time and place the pieces in an electric blender. Blend at high speed and continue adding pieces of potato until the 4 potatoes are well blended. You may have to turn the machine off and on a few times.

Line a large strainer with a paper towel and hook it on a bowl or saucepan. Pour the blended potatoes into the strainer. It's amazing how much liquid will drain off those 4 potatoes. Discard the liquid.

Don't wash or peel mushrooms. Wipe clean with fingers, or damp
118 *paper towel. Cut a thin slice off the bottom of each stem.*

Grate a medium-to-small onion in a large bowl. Add an egg and mix well. Add a teaspoon of salt, $1/8$ teaspoon of pepper, 2 tablespoons of flour, a teaspoon of cornstarch, and a teaspoon of baking powder. Mix it all thoroughly. Empty the drained potatoes over this mixture into the large bowl. Beat it all together until the mixture is smooth.

Thinly slice $1/2$ pound of mushrooms on the large blade of a vegetable grater and fold them into the potato batter.

In a large skillet heat about $1/4$ inch of oil until it is very hot, 375°. Spoon the batter, using a large cooking or serving spoon, into the hot skillet. When the edges are brown and crisp, turn the pancakes over to cook the other side. Add oil so the level will be $1/4$ inch again and repeat.

The Potato Mushroom Pancakes are best if they drain for a minute on paper towels as soon as they are removed from the skillet, and served right away. However, if you must cook all the batter before serving, keep them hot in a warm oven but place them on a rack above a baking sheet. If they are laid flat, they will begin to get rubbery. Serve sour cream or yogurt for dolloping.

POTATO MUSHROOM PUDDING

6 servings

Follow the preceding recipe for Potato Mushroom Pancakes, but instead of frying them pour the batter into a well-greased, 2-quart baking dish. Dribble some oil on top. Bake uncovered in a 375° preheated oven for 50 minutes.

SLICED POTATOES WITH MUSHROOMS

6 servings

This is a lovely way to serve potatoes. The following recipe is based on the French *Pommes de Terre Anna* with mushrooms added. It is usually served unmolded but doesn't have to be. For an embellished version, add a can of truffles sliced very thin along with the mushrooms.

1/2 *lb. mushrooms*
  4 potatoes, medium-large
  4 Tbsp. butter (1/2 stick)
  1 onion, medium-small
    salt and pepper

——————————·•◦◦•·——————————

Peel 4 medium-to-large potatoes and let them sit in very cold water while you slice each one as thinly as possible. Return the slices to the cold water until all have been cut.

Drain the potato slices and dry them. This is most easily done by spreading them out on a dish towel and covering them with another towel. Loosely roll the 2 towels with the potatoes in between.

If you plan to unmold this dish, you must use a flat-bottomed mold; otherwise a casserole will do. Butter a 1 1/2-quart baking dish generously with some of the butter from the half-stick. Arrange a layer of potato slices on the bottom so they overlap neatly. Grate 1/3 of a medium-to-small onion over the potato slices and spread it. Sprinkle with salt and pepper. Slice some mushrooms, not too thin, and arrange them in a layer on the potatoes. Dot with butter, using at least a tablespoon from the half-stick. Repeat the layers.

Arrange some of the potato slices around the sides of the pan, standing on edge and overlapping again. It is all right to squeeze everything to do this—the dish is made more compact.

Continue with the layers of potato and mushrooms, sprinkling

120   *Don't wash or peel mushrooms. Wipe clean with fingers, or damp paper towel. Cut a thin slice off the bottom of each stem.*

with salt and pepper and grated onion. Dot with butter until all the ingredients are used. Cover tightly and bake in a preheated 400° oven for about 1 hour. Test for doneness by piercing the potatoes with the point of a small sharp knife. If they feel tender, the dish is done.

To unmold, tilt the baking pan so the excess butter drains out before you invert the pan onto the serving dish. Surround with parsley.

MUSHROOM TZIMMIS

6 to 8 servings

This is one of those nice dishes to do when the oven is on anyhow. It goes with roasts, especially pork and pot roast.

1 lb. mushrooms
1 lb. carrots
1 sweet potato (1/2 lb.)
4 Tbsp. butter
5 Tbsp. flour
1 cup hot milk

1/2 cup brown sugar, lightly packed
1/4 tsp. nutmeg
1 tsp. salt
1/8 tsp. pepper
1/2 cup orange juice

1 Tbsp. grated lemon rind

———••⌈∞⌋••———

Peel 1 pound of carrots. Cut them into 2-inch lengths. Quarter these lengths, then cut in eighths. This will give thin julienne-type strips. Peel a sweet potato and dice. Place the carrots and potatoes in a large bowl.

In a 1 1/2- or 2-quart saucepan melt 4 tablespoons of butter over low heat. Add 5 tablespoons of flour and cream them together with a wire whisk. Stir while the butter-flour mixture cooks for 2 minutes.

Add 1 cup of hot milk (1/2 cup first, the rest slowly), stirring with the whisk all the time to make the sauce smooth. Stir 1/2 cup of lightly packed brown sugar into the sauce. Add 1/4 teaspoon of nutmeg, one teaspoon of salt, 1/8 teaspoon of pepper, 1/2 cup of orange juice, and the grated rind of half a lemon (1 tablespoon). Stir some more. Remove from heat.

Cut 1 pound of mushrooms into quarters. Add them to the sauce and mix well to make sure all the mushrooms are covered with sauce. Combine the mushrooms and the sauce with the carrots and potatoes. Turn out into a generously buttered 2-quart casserole. Cover. Bake in a preheated 375° oven for 1 hour. Remove the cover and bake for another 1/2 hour.

Don't wash or peel mushrooms. Wipe clean with fingers, or damp
paper towel. Cut a thin slice off the bottom of each stem.

MUSHROOM PUDDING

To make mushroom custard, eliminate the toast.

6 servings

½ lb. mushrooms	⅛ tsp. nutmeg
½ cup egg pastina*	4 slices toast
2 cups milk	3 Tbsp. butter
3 eggs	1 Tbsp. fresh chopped
1 tsp. salt	parsley

———————•◦⋙⋘◦•———————

Boil ½ cup egg pastina in 2 cups of water for 5 minutes. Drain in a strainer and rinse with cold water.

Pour 2 cups of milk into a bowl and beat 3 eggs, 1 teaspoon of salt, and ⅛ teaspoon of nutmeg with the milk. Soak 4 slices of toast (ends are best) in this egg mixture for at least 10 minutes until the slices are thoroughly softened.

Slice ½ pound mushrooms thin and sauté them in a large skillet in 3 tablespoons of butter. Sprinkle a tablespoon of freshly chopped parsley over the mushrooms.

Generously butter a 7- or 8-inch-square baking pan. Lay the soaked slices of toast in the buttered pan. Arrange the sliced sautéed mushrooms on them and cover the mushrooms with the cooked, drained pastina. Pour the remaining egg-milk liquid over all and dot the top with extra butter. Bake in a preheated 350° oven for 35 minutes.

Serve this pudding instead of potatoes or rice. Cut it in squares and add a dollop of sour cream or yogurt. A square can also be served on top of a plain cooked vegetable, such as spinach, peas, or string beans.

*Found next to spaghetti in supermarkets.

Salads

MUSHROOM SALADS

Fresh mushrooms in a green salad always taste springlike, even in the middle of winter. They go with any fresh salad vegetables. They can also be combined with cooked vegetables, such as string beans, asparagus, artichokes, bean sprouts, red kidney beans, or eggplant. The fresh mushrooms may be whole, halved, quartered, sliced, or chopped.

Any salad dressing, sauce, or mayonnaise may be used. The best dressed mushroom salad uses fresh chervil, basil, or tarragon, but since these fine herbs are not often available, the dried ones are a very good second best.

My favorite fresh mushroom salad is a simple one. The mushrooms are sliced fine on the large blade of a vegetable grater, tossed with greens, and dressed with the following:

FRESH MUSHROOM DRESSING

½ cup dressing

½ cup oil	pepper, fresh ground
2 Tbsp. lemon juice	¼ tsp. dry mustard
1 tsp. dry wine	¼ tsp. chervil
½ tsp. salt	¼ tsp. basil
	¼ tsp. tarragon

Place all the ingredients in a screw-top jar. Shake vigorously until everything is well blended. A temporary emulsion will form. Pour the dressing over the salad before it separates.

MARINATED MUSHROOM SALADS

Use Marinated Mushrooms (see Index) in a tossed green salad, in a fresh vegetable salad and add hard-cooked eggs, in a cooked vegetable salad, in a chef salad, and as a garnish for main-dish salads.

MARINATED VEGETABLE SALAD

This salad is an especially good one to use for buffets. It doesn't use greens, therefore doesn't wilt, and it can be made in advance. Sitting at room temperature for hours doesn't hurt it a bit. Follow the directions for Marinated Mushrooms. Use the marinade as salad dressing. In a large bowl combine the marinated mushrooms with any combination of the following:

cauliflower buds (especially recommended because they remain
   crisp and add to the variety of textures)
broccoli buds
cherry tomatoes
olives, green or black
artichoke hearts
cucumber slices
chick peas
avocado
celery (1-inch pieces)

CHRISTMAS MUSHROOM SALAD

Combine Marinated Mushrooms, red cherry tomatoes, and fresh green broccoli buds in the marinade the mushrooms were cooked in. Not only is this a delicious and very pretty red-and-green salad, but it also has the advantage of gracefully maintaining its flavor and appearance even after sitting for many hours on an "open house" party table. It goes superbly with ham.

Don't wash or peel mushrooms. Wipe clean with fingers, or damp
128   *paper towel. Cut a thin slice off the bottom of each stem.*

MUSHROOM POTATO SALAD

2 quarts

If you've never eaten mushrooms raw, this is a good way to begin. The mushrooms become marinated in the potato salad. Not only is their taste refreshing, but strangely enough, they also add a nutlike flavor.

1 lb. mushrooms
7 medium potatoes (2 lbs.)
1¼ cups mayonnaise*
1 large green pepper, diced
2 scallions, including green, sliced thin
1 sour pickle, chopped fine

2 sweet gherkins, chopped fine
3 hard-cooked eggs, sliced
½ tsp. salt
½ tsp. dill weed
½ tsp. chervil
⅛ tsp. black pepper

Wash 7 potatoes and boil them in water to cover until they are tender. Drain them.

While the potatoes are boiling, prepare everything else.

Combine in a large bowl: 1¼ cups mayonnaise; 1 pound of mushrooms (chopped chunk style); 1 large diced green pepper; 2 scallions, including the green, sliced thin; 1 sour pickle and 2 sweet gherkins, both chopped fine; 3 hard-cooked eggs, sliced; ½ teaspoon each of salt, dill weed, and chervil; and ⅛ teaspoon of black pepper. Mix everything well.

When the potatoes are cool enough to handle, peel them and cut into large dice. Combine them with the other vegetables.

If this Mushroom Potato Salad is to be unmolded, pack it into a 2-quart bowl or mold while it is warm, pressing it down firmly with the back of a large spoon. Cover and chill overnight. Unmold the next day.

*Mushroom Mayonnaise adds still another dimension to this potato salad.

MUSHROOM SLAW

4 to 6 servings

Fresh, uncooked mushrooms can turn an ordinary cole slaw into an exceptional one.

1/4 lb. mushrooms
1/2 cup mayonnaise*
 4 cups shredded cabbage
1/2 dill pickle, finely chopped
 1 sweet gherkin, finely
     chopped
1/8 tsp. chervil
1/8 tsp. dill weed
1/4 tsp. salt
   pepper

———————————•⋘∞⋙•———————————

Slice 1/4 pound of mushrooms fine on the large blade of a vegetable grater. Combine them in a large bowl with 1/2 cup of mayonnaise.

Add 4 cups of shredded cabbage, 1/2 dill pickle and I sweet gherkin, both finely chopped, and mix. Add 1/8 teaspoon each of chervil and dill weed, 1/4 teaspoon of salt, and a few turns of the pepper mill. Mix again and let the mushroom slaw "rest" for at least 10 minutes before serving.

*If homemade mayonnaise is used for this cole slaw, it will, of course, be much better than store-bought. And if you want it to be *really* outstanding, use Mushroom Mayonnaise (see Index).

Don't wash or peel mushrooms. Wipe clean with fingers, or damp paper towel. Cut a thin slice off the bottom of each stem.

RITUAL RELISH

2 cups relish

Food has played a very special role in celebrating significant occasions throughout all known human history. Every ingredient in this recipe has a long-established symbolic and ritualistic significance. One has only to think of Eve's apple, blood-red wine, anointing oil, germinating wheat, the saving salt, and so on. Mushrooms are used in some of the world's most exotic rituals, and they also add an exotic touch to the following recipe. This is a wonderful relish to eat with pork chops or pot roast. It is also very good with cooked greens and makes a superb salad with raw ones.

$1/2$ lb. mushrooms
$1/4$ cup dry red wine
$1/4$ cup oil
  2 Tbsp. lemon juice
$1/2$ tsp. salt
  1 large apple
  3 Tbsp. wheat germ
  2 hard-cooked eggs

Combine in a medium-size bowl $1/4$ cup dry red wine, $1/4$ cup oil, 2 tablespoons of lemon juice, and $1/2$ teaspoon of salt.

Peel and dice fine one large apple. Add.

Slice $1/2$ pound of very fresh, firm mushrooms on the large blade of a vegetable grater, then chop. Add to the bowl and sprinkle them with 3 tablespoons of wheat germ. Stir.

Chop, not too fine, 2 hard-cooked eggs and mix them in.

GAZPACHO ASPIC

6 to 8 servings

Gazpacho, the cold Spanish soup, makes a fine molded mushroom salad.

$1/4$ lb. mushrooms
    Gazpacho recipe (see Index)
$1 1/2$ Tbsp. unflavored gelatin ($1 1/2$ envelopes)

Prepare and chop the vegetables in the Gazpacho recipe. Add another $1/4$ pound of mushrooms.

Use the $2 1/2$ cups of vegetable juice to make aspic. Soften $1 1/2$ tablespoons of unflavored gelatin in $1/2$ cup of vegetable juice. Bring 2 cups of juice to a boil. Remove from heat. Pour the softened gelatin into the hot juice. Stir while it dissolves. Refrigerate the juice until it begins to thicken a little. Fold everything in the Gazpacho recipe into the gelatin. (If the solids are added before the aspic begins to thicken, they'll rise to the top.)

Pour this mixture into a bowl, mold, or individual molds and chill until firm, about 3 hours.

Sauces

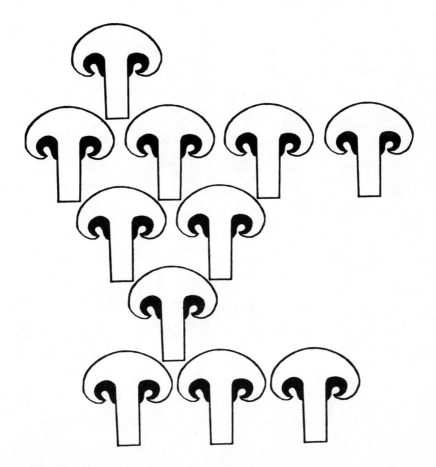

MUSHROOM SAUCES

Mushroom sauces are a very special part of mushroom cooking. They are easy to make, taking only about 10 minutes. The small investment of time for the enormous amount of pleasure a mushroom sauce gives is one of those lucky breaks in life. A plain broiled veal chop, chicken, or fish becomes a special delicacy with a mushroom sauce spooned over it. The old saying that a well-made sauce can change an ordinary cook into a fine one is especially true of mushroom sauces. No can of cream-of-mushroom soup, no matter how expensive, is a suitable substitute for a mushroom sauce which you yourself can make in a matter of minutes.

Two Utensils

For most mushroom sauces, as for most other sauces, there are two absolutely essential utensils—a heavy-bottomed saucepan and a wire whisk. Sauces scorch easily in lightweight pans, even if they are carefully and constantly stirred. Heavy metal holds and distributes the heat evenly. The saucepan should be slightly rounded at its base to permit the wire whisk to do its job of blending. A fine quality sauce should be

thoroughly blended
have a smooth texture
and a light consistency

The wire whisk is the tool that can turn a gravy into a sauce. It gets rid of the lumps and does the blending and smoothing. A $1\frac{1}{2}$-quart saucepan is the best size for making 2 cups of mushroom sauce.

SAUCE INSURANCE

If a national cooking characteristic exists in the United States, it is speed. Speed is not automatically a negative quality, but it is frequently carried too far. Americans have become so accustomed to "one bowl, one step" methods for "fast gourmet" dishes that they sometimes seem to have been subliminally conditioned to skip steps. For example, in order to save washing another pot some cooks will use cold milk instead of hot when preparing a sauce. A false economy indeed, for the time saved in pot washing must then be used in additional beating to achieve the proper smoothness, since cold milk does not immediately dissolve the flour-butter mixture.

Most sauces are made by using low heat. If it ever becomes a question, play it safe and slow, with low heat. High heat will shrivel the grains of starch in the flour, thereby destroying the possibility of smooth texture.

Stock and Broth

The words stock and broth are used interchangeably these days. There is no question about homemade stock being the most desirable for making sauces. However, since it is unrealistic to assume the average kitchen refrigerator houses the basic stocks, the next best thing should be used. The dehydrated powdered broths are superior to the cubes and canned liquids. Their use makes a lot of practical sense, especially for working people who choose to do their own cooking. Among the powders available, the quality varies a great deal. The best on the market currently is the MBT chicken broth and prime broth, which is beef flavored.

Cooking the Food in the Sauce

Food can be cooked in the sauce, but only for a short time. The mushrooms should not be overcooked. For example, when cooking green lima or string beans, add them to Basic Mushroom Sauce I for the last 5 minutes of their cooking time. Or in the case of fish or chicken, spoon the sauce over the cooked food and return it to the oven or under a broiler for browning. A sauce browned over food in this way is called "glazed."

Don't wash or peel mushrooms. Wipe clean with fingers, or damp
136   *paper towel. Cut a thin slice off the bottom of each stem.*

Shallots and Onions

Shallots, onions, green onions, or scallions (white and green parts) may be added to any mushroom sauce. They should be cooked until soft only, not browned. Cook them in the butter before it is combined with the flour. Since mushroom sauces naturally have texture from the mushroom slices, it is not necessary to strain the sauce to remove the shallots or onions. But if you want, strain the sauce before adding the mushrooms.

Storing

If a sauce is made in the morning for use in the evening, it may be stored in the refrigerator, covered, in the saucepan in which it was cooked, and warmed very slowly when needed. Cover the sauce as soon as it is cooked; this will help to prevent a hard skin from forming. After the sauce has cooled, float a little milk, cream, sherry, or vermouth on the top before refrigerating. A mushroom sauce may be kept for a couple of days in the refrigerator in a tightly covered container. It will become quite firm and should be heated either in a double boiler or a saucepan. (If in a saucepan, add a little liquid: milk, water, stock, or wine.) Use low heat and stir with a wire whisk.

Mushroom sauces freeze very well. It is best to let them defrost at room temperature.

BASIC MUSHROOM SAUCE I

White Sauce

This white mushroom sauce is one of the most important recipes in mushroom cooking. It can literally become over 100 different things. It is the simplest of sauces, containing flour, butter, and milk. It makes a fine dish served by itself on toast or with crackers, and becomes enriched with such additions as hard-cooked egg slices, ham, tuna, or salmon. It is the perfect sauce for vegetables, fish, shellfish, veal, and poultry.

White Mushroom Sauce

2 generous cups sauce

$\frac{1}{2}$ lb. mushrooms	4 Tbsp. butter ($\frac{1}{2}$ stick)	$\frac{1}{2}$ tsp. salt
2 cups milk	3 Tbsp. flour	$\frac{1}{8}$ tsp. white pepper

Heat 2 cups of milk almost to boiling.

In a $1\frac{1}{2}$- or 2-quart saucepan melt 2 tablespoons of butter over low heat. Add 3 tablespoons of flour, and cream them together with a wire whisk. Cook this butter-flour mixture for 2 minutes. Keep stirring with the whisk so it does not brown.

Add 2 cups of hot milk (a half-cup first, then the rest slowly), stirring with the whisk all the time to make the sauce smooth. Beat the sauce for about 3 minutes and then let it simmer. Stir with the whisk from time to time.

While the sauce is simmering, slice $\frac{1}{2}$ pound mushrooms fine on the large blade of a vegetable grater. In a large skillet (12-inch size is best) heat 2 tablespoons of butter until bubbly. Cook the mushroom slices over moderately high heat for about 3 minutes. Stir them often and be careful not to allow them to lump together. Quite a bit of steam will escape.

Add the mushrooms to the simmering sauce. Use a rubber scraper to get all the butter out of the frying pan into the sauce. Stir and let simmer for 2 more minutes. Add $\frac{1}{2}$ teaspoon of salt and $\frac{1}{8}$ teaspoon of white pepper. One or more of the following seasonings may also be added:

Chopped fresh parsley, chives, or watercress
Chopped and sautéed shallots, garlic, onions, or scallions
A teaspoon of lemon juice or Worcestershire sauce
Some slivers of cooked ham
A tablespoon of capers
$\frac{1}{8}$ teaspoon of basil, cardamon, chervil, coriander, dill, dry mustard, fennel, ginger, mace, marjoram, nutmeg, savory, tarragon, or thyme
A tablespoon of dry white wine, sherry, brandy, or dry vermouth.

Don't wash or peel mushrooms. Wipe clean with fingers, or damp paper towel. Cut a thin slice off the bottom of each stem.

BASIC MUSHROOM SAUCE II

Stock Sauce

2 generous cups sauce

¹/₂ lb. mushrooms	4 Tbsp. butter (¹/₂ stick)
2 cups chicken, meat, or fish stock	3 Tbsp. flour
	salt and pepper

Follow the directions for Sauce I but use 2 cups of chicken, meat, or fish stock instead of 2 cups of milk. Add salt and pepper by taste because the amount of seasoning in the stock will determine how much is needed.

SUPREME MUSHROOM SAUCE

Follow the directions for Basic Sauce II, using chicken stock, but instead of 2 cups, use only 1¹/₂ cups. Replace the other ¹/₂ cup of stock with heavy cream. The cream is added to the sauce at the end, after the mushrooms. The sauce should be heated until it barely begins to simmer then should immediately be removed from the heat.

ENRICHED MUSHROOM SAUCE

Enriched mushroom sauce is Basic Sauce I with the addition of 2 teaspoons of dehydrated chicken broth during the simmer stage.

Ordinarily a rich sauce has to be cooked for a long time in order to reduce the liquid and achieve the proper density of flavor. This enriched mushroom sauce is reduced at the outset by using 2 teaspoons of dehydrated broth and eliminating 2 cups of liquid.

MUSHROOM CREAM SAUCE

Follow the directions for Basic Sauce I and replace some or all of the milk with cream.

BASIC MUSHROOM SAUCE II WITH WINE ADDED

Replace 1/2 cup of stock with 1/2 cup of wine. If a light sauce is desired, use 1 1/2 cups of chicken stock and 1/2 cup of dry white wine. For a dark sauce, use 1 1/2 cups of beef stock and 1/2 cup dry red wine.

FINE HERB MUSHROOM SAUCE

Follow the directions for Basic Mushroom Sauce II, using chicken stock. Replace 1/2 cup of chicken stock with 1/2 cup of dry white wine and add 1 teaspoon each of chopped chives and fresh chopped parsley and 1/4 teaspoon each of tarragon and chervil. Before serving stir in a teaspoon of lemon juice.

MUSHROOM CHEESE SAUCE

Especially good for shrimp and scallops or as a hot dip.

Basic Mushroom Sauce 1, page 137
1/2 *cup shredded mild cheddar, Swiss, or Gruyère cheese*
cayenne

Follow the directions for Basic Mushroom Sauce I and before adding the mushrooms, add 1/2 cup of shredded cheese. Stir, and when the cheese is melted, add the mushroom slices. Sprinkle with one dash of cayenne pepper.

Don't wash or peel mushrooms. Wipe clean with fingers, or damp
paper towel. Cut a thin slice off the bottom of each stem.

MAGYAR MUSHROOM SAUCE

2½ cups sauce

Spoon this sauce over broiled or baked chicken served with broad noodles. It can also be used for veal, lamb, or pork chops.

½ lb. mushrooms	2 Tbsp. flour
1 cup milk	1 Tbsp. paprika
4 Tbsp. butter	½ tsp. salt
2 Tbsp. chopped onion	⅛ tsp. pepper
1 cup sour cream (½ pt.)	

———◦◦◦———

Heat a cup of milk almost to boiling.

In a 1½- or 2-quart saucepan melt 2 tablespoons of butter over low heat. Cook 2 tablespoons of chopped onion in the butter until it is softened (almost translucent, but not brown). Add 2 tablespoons of flour and stir with a wire whisk. Cook for 2 minutes. Keep stirring with the whisk so it does not brown.

Add 1 cup of milk (a half-cup first and the rest slowly), stirring with the whisk all the time to make the sauce smooth. Add 1 tablespoon of paprika, ½ teaspoon of salt, and ⅛ teaspoon of pepper. Beat the sauce for about 3 minutes and then let it simmer, using the lowest heat possible, for the sauce is thick.

While the sauce is simmering, cut ½ pound mushrooms in quarters. In a large skillet heat 2 tablespoons of butter until bubbly and sauté the mushrooms over moderately high heat for about 2 or 3 minutes, stirring most of the time.

Add the mushrooms to the simmering sauce and stir. Remove from heat and stir in 1 cup sour cream, which is at room temperature. Be sure the food this sauce is spooned over is very hot, for the cream will cool down the sauce a little.

MUSHROOM MAYONNAISE

3 cups mayonnaise

This is an unusual mayonnaise. It can also be used as a dip. Because it is made in an electric blender, it doesn't take much time. As a dressing for a sliced fresh mushroom salad, it's perfect. Use it as you would any other mayonnaise.

1/4 lb. mushrooms
2 eggs
1 tsp. salt
1/2 tsp. dry mustard
2 Tbsp. lemon juice
1 1/2 cups oil

Break 2 whole eggs into an electric blender jar. Add 1 teaspoon of salt and 1/2 teaspoon of mustard. Cover and blend for 1/2 minute at highest speed. (Use the highest speed throughout this recipe.)

Add 2 tablespoons of lemon juice and turn the blender on and off.

The oil should always be added in a thin slow stream, or in drops. Turn the blender on and begin adding the oil. After about 1/2 cup of oil has been added, the mayonnaise will begin to thicken and form a whirlpool in the center. Continue dripping the oil in and with the other hand drop a mushroom into the center of the whirlpool. If the mushrooms are large, cut them in half. Continue adding the oil slowly and continue adding the mushrooms, one at a time.

Do not add a mushroom until the last one has become incorporated into the mayonnaise. If the oil, or a mushroom, remains on top of the mayonnaise and the whirlpool has disappeared, replace the cover and turn the blender off. When you turn it on again, the whirlpool will again appear. Continue adding the oil and mushrooms until all are used. Refrigerate in a covered container and use cold. It will keep for almost a week.

Don't wash or peel mushrooms. Wipe clean with fingers, or damp
paper towel. Cut a thin slice off the bottom of each stem.

MUSHROOM COTTAGE CHEESE SAUCE

2 cups sauce

There are times when one wants a sauce that is not rich, but is nevertheless delicious. This is such a sauce. It is most versatile and can be used either hot or cold. It is not a "mock" mayonnaise or a "mock" hollandaise. It is itself, a very practical mushroom sauce which can be substituted for other, heavier sauces. Served warm on asparagus or broccoli, it's terrific. Served cold on a salad, it's a delightful change. For fish and chicken, use it hot or cold.

Be careful to use low heat when preparing this sauce, for it uses egg yolks and lemon juice, a combination which curdles when overheated.

1/2 lb. mushrooms	1 tsp. dry mustard
1 cup cottage cheese	1/2 tsp. salt
2 Tbsp. lemon juice	1/8 tsp. freshly ground black
2 egg yolks	pepper
dash of cayenne	

Place all the ingredients except the mushrooms in a blender and turn it on at high speed. Turn it on and off a couple of times and scrape the sides to be sure everything is blended.

Drop a mushroom into the whirlpool that forms in the center of the sauce. When the mushroom disappears, drop another, and so on until 1/2 pound of mushrooms is used.

Pour this mixture into the top of a double boiler or in a heavy-bottomed saucepan. Use the lowest heat possible—the absolute lowest. Use a wire whisk to stir it, not that it needs beating, but the whisk gets everything blended nicely. After a couple of minutes it will begin to thicken. Stir it all the time, and just before it begins to boil, quickly remove from the heat and empty into another container. Do not let this sauce cool in the pan it was cooked in, for it could curdle from the heat of the pan.

VELVET MUSHROOM SAUCE

2 cups sauce

A sauce made with egg yolks and heavy cream produces a delicacy that no other combination of ingredients can match. The embellishment of mushrooms floating through the velvety smoothness really makes this sauce outstanding. Use it for fish, shellfish, veal, or poultry, particularly Cornish hens.

1/2 lb. mushrooms
4 Tbsp. butter
3 Tbsp. flour
1 1/2 cups hot chicken broth
2 egg yolks
1/2 cup heavy cream
1/2 tsp. salt
1/8 tsp. white pepper
1 Tbsp. lemon juice

Slice 1/2 pound of mushrooms fine on the large blade of a vegetable grater. Sauté them in 2 tablespoons of butter in a large skillet for 3 minutes. Reserve, uncovered.

In a 1 1/2- or 2-quart saucepan melt 2 tablespoons of butter over low heat. Add 3 tablespoons of flour and cream them together with a wire whisk. Cook for 2 minutes. Keep stirring with the whisk so this flour-butter mixture does not brown.

Add 1 1/2 cups of hot chicken broth (a half-cup first and the rest slowly), stirring with the whisk all the time to make the sauce smooth. Beat the sauce and then let it simmer, still using the same low heat.

Don't wash or peel mushrooms. Wipe clean with fingers, or damp paper towel. Cut a thin slice off the bottom of each stem.

Mix 2 egg yolks with $1/2$ cup of heavy cream in a bowl. Beat in some of the hot sauce, about a tablespoon at a time until about a half-cup has been used. Pour this egg-cream mixture into the sauce pot slowly, in a thin stream, beating it in as you pour.

Allow the sauce to simmer for a minute and then add the mushroom slices. Use a rubber scraper to get all the mushroom butter into the sauce. Add $1/2$ teaspoon salt and $1/8$ teaspoon white pepper. Remove from the heat and add a tablespoon of lemon juice.

MUSHROOM WINE SAUCES

These mushroom wine sauces are very easy to make. They are the best ones for beginners because the ritual of the *roux* (combining butter and flour) has been eliminated and there is no cream, lemon juice, or egg yolk, therefore no danger of curdling. These sauces can be kept in the refrigerator for a few days in tightly covered containers, and they also freeze well.

The red and white wine mushroom sauces which follow have an international quality, gastronomically speaking. They combine elements of the two greatest traditions in cooking, the French and the Chinese. From the French there is the refinement of cooking in wine. Escoffier, the greatest name in French gastronomy, favored the use of cornstarch as a thickening agent because he felt it produced a lighter sauce; and cornstarch is an integral part of Chinese cooking, which is so much admired because of its lightness and digestibility.

Try the Red Wine Mushroom Sauce on a broiled hamburger and you'll see for yourself. The same red sauce can grace a fine slice of beef filet equally well. Use the White Wine Mushroom Sauce on chicken, fish, veal, sweetbreads, or brains.

RED WINE MUSHROOM SAUCE

1⅔ cups sauce

½ lb. mushrooms
1 cup dry red wine
1 cup strong beef broth
½ tsp. salt

⅛ tsp. freshly ground pepper
⅛ tsp. tarragon
2 scant Tbsp. cornstarch
2 Tbsp. butter

Bring 1 cup of dry red wine to a boil in a 1½- or 2-quart saucepan, using medium heat. Let the wine boil for 5 minutes.

Slice ½ pound of mushrooms fine on the largest blade of a vegetable grater and cook the slices in the boiling wine for about 5 minutes. The wine will gradually be reduced.

While the mushrooms are cooking, raise the heat a little, and as the wine bubbles up on the sides, some froth will form in the center. Spoon this off and discard. Return the heat to medium. Do this about four times.

Add 1 cup of strong beef stock, ½ teaspoon of salt, ⅛ teaspoon of freshly ground black pepper, and ⅛ teaspoon of tarragon. Stir.

In a small bowl mix 2 scant tablespoons of cornstarch with 2 tablespoons of water to make a thin paste. Pour this into the sauce and stir.

Add 1 tablespoon of butter and swirl it into the sauce with a fork. After it is thoroughly incorporated, add another tablespoon of butter and do the same thing. Remove the sauce from the heat. If it is not going to be used right away, cover the saucepan to avoid the formation of a skin on top.

The beginner might ask why not use less wine instead of wasting time boiling it away. The answer is taste. The thing we're after is the concentrated wine flavor without the alcohol taste or the volume of liquid.

Don't wash or peel mushrooms. Wipe clean with fingers, or damp
146   paper towel. Cut a thin slice off the bottom of each stem.

WHITE WINE MUSHROOM SAUCE

1⅔ *cups sauce*

 ½ lb. mushrooms
  1 cup dry white wine
  1 cup strong chicken broth
 ½ tsp. salt
 ⅛ tsp. white pepper
 ¼ tsp. chervil
  2 scant Tbsp. cornstarch
  2 Tbsp. butter

------------◦◦◦◦◦◦◦◦------------

Bring I cup of dry white wine to a boil in a 1½- or 2-quart saucepan, using medium heat. Let the wine boil for 5 minutes.

Slice ½ pound of mushrooms fine on the largest blade of a vegetable grater and cook the slices in the boiling wine for about 5 minutes. The wine is gradually being reduced.

While the mushrooms are cooking, raise the heat a little, and as the wine bubbles up on the sides, some froth will form in the center. Spoon this off and discard. Return the heat to medium. Do this about four times.

Add I cup of strong chicken stock, ½ teaspoon of salt, ⅛ teaspoon of white pepper, and ¼ teaspoon of chervil. Stir.

In a small bowl mix 2 scant tablespoons of cornstarch with 2 tablespoons of water to make a thin paste. Pour this into the sauce and stir.

Add I tablespoon of butter and swirl it into the sauce with a fork. After it is thoroughly incorporated, add another tablespoon of butter and do the same thing. Remove the sauce from the heat. If it is not going to be used right away, cover the saucepan to avoid the formation of a skin on top.

MADEIRA MUSHROOM SAUCE

Follow the directions for Basic Mushroom Sauce II, adding a finely chopped shallot or some chopped scallions to the melted butter. Cook 1 minute. Add $1/2$ tablespoon more flour. Cook the butter-flour mixture for 2 additional minutes until it becomes golden brown. Use $11/2$ cups of strong meat stock instead of 2. Add $1/3$ cup Madeira or dry sherry after adding the stock. Follow the same directions for the mushrooms. Use this sauce for meat, especially steak, liver, and ham.

MUSHROOM DUXELLES SAUCE

Any sauce in this chapter may be used as the basis for a duxelles sauce. Duxelles refers to the treatment of the mushrooms—chopped fine. See Index for preparing the mushrooms in the duxelles manner. Add them in the same way you would add the sliced mushrooms in any of the sauce recipes.

MUSHROOM PURÉE SAUCE

Mushroom Purée (see Index) can be used as a sauce. Although it will gracefully adorn anything over which it is spooned, it is, as sauces go, thick. It may be thinned down by adding $1/2$ cup cream or broth.

TRUFFLE SAUCES

Truffles, finely chopped or thinly sliced, may be added to any of the mushroom sauces or can replace the mushrooms. If they are fresh, peel them and sauté with, or instead of, the mushrooms. If they are canned, they may be sautéed, but it isn't necessary. They can be added to the sauce for the last 2 minutes of cooking. (For more information about truffles, see Index.)

Don't wash or peel mushrooms. Wipe clean with fingers, or damp
148 *paper towel. Cut a thin slice off the bottom of each stem.*

MUSHROOM SPAGHETTI SAUCE

This is a thick sauce. If a thinner one is desired, add another 1/4 cup of water. It is enough for one pound of spaghetti. Mushroom meat balls go well with this sauce.

1/2 lb. mushrooms	1/2 tsp. oregano
1 clove garlic	1/2 tsp. basil
1 can tomato purée (10 oz.)*	1/2 tsp. salt
1 can tomato paste (6 oz.)	1/8 tsp. pepper
2 Tbsp. olive oil	1/2 tsp. sugar

1/4 cup water

———◄∞►———

Slice the mushrooms. Mince the clove of garlic, then mash it.

Put all the ingredients in a saucepan and mix. Bring to a quick boil and lower the heat. Gently simmer the sauce 5 to 7 minutes, covered.

MUSHROOM ESSENCE

Mushroom Essence is the cooking liquid from stewed mushrooms or canned mushrooms which has been rapidly boiled down to less than one-fourth its original volume. It is syrupy, and used to flavor vegetables and sauces. It should be stored in an airtight jar and can be kept in the refrigerator for a few days or in the freezer for many months.

---

*If your supermarket doesn't carry the 10-ounce size, use a larger one and taste the sauce. You may need more salt or another dash of oregano or basil.

MUSHROOM GARLIC SAUCE

4 to 6 servings

This is a robust sauce, yet for all its pungency, it is also very delicate. It is best served on green spaghetti but it is also very good on ordinary spaghetti. There is enough sauce for one pound of pasta.

1/2 lb. mushrooms
6 Tbsp. olive oil
8 cloves garlic
1 large green pepper
1 tsp. salt
1/8 tsp. freshly ground black
     pepper
  Romano cheese, grated

Chop 8 cloves of garlic fine. Cut 1 large green pepper into small dice.

Chop 1/2 pound of mushrooms fine.

Heat 6 tablespoons of olive oil in a 12-inch skillet over moderately high heat. Sauté the pepper and garlic for 2 minutes, stirring once or twice. Add the chopped mushrooms and sauté for 3 minutes, stirring often.

Sprinkle with 1 teaspoon of salt and 1/8 teaspoon of freshly ground black pepper. Serve on spaghetti and sprinkle each serving generously with grated Romano cheese.

Don't wash or peel mushrooms. Wipe clean with fingers, or damp paper towel. Cut a thin slice off the bottom of each stem.

MUSHROOM BUTTER

1 scant cup

This is a versatile compound butter. It can be used as a spread, spooned into baked potatoes, added to cooked vegetables, spread over fish, steak or poultry, or spooned into a plain sauce to enrich it. A plain broiled hamburger becomes a fancy one when spread with mushroom butter. The butter can be kept in the refrigerator for a week in a tightly covered container. It also freezes well.

1/4 lb. mushrooms
1/4 lb. butter
 2 Tbsp. butter

Have 1/4 pound of butter at room temperature.

Shred 1/4 pound of mushrooms, then chop a little, or put them through a meat grinder, using the finest blade. Cook the mushrooms in a large skillet in 2 tablespoons of additional butter over moderately high heat for 5 minutes. Stir them frequently to permit more steam to escape. Let them cool. (If the mushrooms are added to the softened butter directly from the hot skillet, the butter will melt and an oily taste will result.)

Whip the butter with a wire whisk for a few minutes to make it fluffy. Add the cooled mushrooms, blending them in well.

Additions: Parboil a tablespoon of minced shallots, scallions, or onions in a little water for 2 minutes. Strain and dry on a paper towel. Add to the mushroom butter. Or add a teaspoon of chopped chives or chervil, or a tablespoon of chopped fresh parsley.

Mushroom Stuffing, Duxelles, Breads, and Fluting

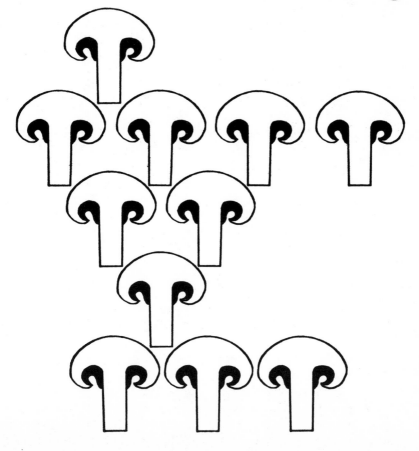

MUSHROOM STUFFING

Mushrooms make stuffings more delicate. They also add fragrance. Ordinarily mushrooms should not be cooked long, but when they are used in stuffings they are protected from direct heat by being encased by fowl, fish, or meat and can withstand the required baking time without overcooking and excessive shrinkage.

Stuffings should always be packed lightly. There must be room for expansion. Never try to force an extra amount into a cavity simply because it is on hand. Instead, bake the leftover quantity separately in a buttered dish.

The following recipes are for stuffing 5 or 6 pounds of fowl, meat, or fish, except for the wild rice recipe, which stuffs 4 pounds. If a 10- or 12-pound turkey is to be stuffed, double the recipe. If a 3-pound chicken, sea bass, or breast of veal is to be stuffed, cut the recipe in half.

Mushroom stuffing becomes mushroom dressing if it is baked in an uncovered, buttered baking dish for 1 hour in a preheated 375° oven.

MUSHROOM BREAD STUFFING

Stuffing for 5 or 6 pounds of chicken, turkey, meat, or fish

1/2 lb. mushrooms
3 cups dried bread, small
   chunks or large crumbs
8 Tbsp. butter (1/4 lb.)
2 Tbsp. minced onion
1/3 cup chopped celery
2 Tbsp. chopped parsley

1/4 tsp. sage
1/4 tsp. thyme
1/4 tsp. marjoram
1/2 tsp. salt
  pepper
1 cup chicken broth
1 egg

If you don't have dried-out bread, toast some and let it air on a rack. Don't cube the bread first and then toast it, for the knife will squeeze together the natural air holes of the bread. Those air holes help keep the stuffing light. Break the dried bread into large pieces and press down on them with a flat-bottomed glass to make small chunks or large crumbs.

Slice 1/2 pound of mushrooms on the large blade of a vegetable grater. Heat 4 tablespoons of butter in a large skillet until it begins to spatter. Sauté over half of the sliced mushrooms for 3 minutes, stirring often, and remove them to a large bowl. Heat 4 more tablespoons of butter and sauté the remaining mushrooms with 2 tablespoons of minced onion and 1/3 cup of chopped celery. Remove to the bowl, using a rubber scraper to get everything.

Sprinkle the mushroom mixture with 2 tablespoons of fresh chopped parsley, 1/4 teaspoon each of sage, thyme, and marjoram, 1/2 teaspoon of salt, and some turns of the pepper mill. Mix.

Pour 1 cup of chicken broth into another large bowl. Toss 3 cups of dried bread into the broth. Toss until the liquid has become absorbed.

Beat an egg and add it to the mushroom mixture. Combine the moistened bread with the mushrooms.

Don't wash or peel mushrooms. Wipe clean with fingers, or damp
156 *paper towel. Cut a thin slice off the bottom of each stem.*

MUSHROOM KASHA STUFFING

Stuffing for 5 or 6 pounds of poultry, meat, or fish

Kasha is made from roasted brown buckwheat groats. Groats are near rice on the shelves of most supermarkets.

$\frac{1}{2}$ lb. mushrooms
1 egg
2 cups water
1 tsp. salt
8 Tbsp. butter ($\frac{1}{4}$ lb.)
2 Tbsp. finely chopped onion
1 small green pepper
1 cup uncooked medium
     groats
1 bay leaf

In a bowl whip an egg with 2 cups of water and 1 teaspoon of salt.

Melt 4 tablespoons of butter in a 3-quart saucepan over moderately high heat. Sauté 2 tablespoons of finely chopped onion and a small diced green pepper for 3 minutes. Lower the heat to moderate and add 1 cup of medium groats. Stir continuously for 3 more minutes.

Add the egg-water and bay leaf. Bring to a boil, cover, and cook over the lowest heat for 15 minutes. Remove the bay leaf and discard.

While the kasha is cooking, slice $\frac{1}{2}$ pound of mushrooms fine on the large blade of a vegetable grater. Heat 4 tablespoons of butter in a large skillet until it begins to spatter. Sauté the mushrooms for 3 minutes, stirring often. Remove to a large bowl.

Combine the mushrooms with the kasha.

MUSHROOM RICE STUFFING

Stuffing for 5 or 6 pounds of poultry, meat, or fish

1/2 lb. mushrooms	1/2 tsp. salt
3 cups cooked rice	1/2 tsp. thyme
5 Tbsp. butter	1/4 tsp. nutmeg
2 scallions, chopped	pepper
1/3 cup chopped celery	1/2 cup chicken or beef broth
2 Tbsp. chopped parsley	1 Tbsp. lemon juice

Slice 1/2 pound of mushrooms on the large blade of a vegetable grater. Heat 3 tablespoons of butter in a large skillet until it begins to spatter. Sauté over half of the sliced mushrooms for 3 minutes, stirring often, and remove them to a large bowl. Heat 2 more tablespoons of butter and sauté the remaining mushrooms with 2 chopped scallions and 1/3 cup chopped celery. Remove to the bowl.

Add 3 cups of cooked rice (it should be firm, not soft) and 2 tablespoons of chopped parsley, 1/2 teaspoon each of salt and thyme, 1/4 teaspoon of nutmeg, a few turns of the pepper mill, 1/2 cup of stock, and 1 tablespoon of lemon juice. Stir everything together lightly.

MUSHROOM POTATO STUFFING

Stuffing for 5 or 6 pounds of poultry, meat, or fish

Follow the directions for Mushroom Bread Stuffing but use only 2 cups of dried bread and 2/3 cup chicken broth. Grate 2 medium potatoes or cut them into cubes and blend in an electric blender. Line a large strainer with a paper towel and let the potatoes drain for 5 minutes. Combine the drained potatoes with the other ingredients.

Don't wash or peel mushrooms. Wipe clean with fingers, or damp paper towel. Cut a thin slice off the bottom of each stem.

WILD RICE MUSHROOM STUFFING

Stuffing for 3 Cornish hens, 4-pound chicken, or 4-pound fish

1/2 lb. mushrooms	1/2 cup sliced almonds
2 cups cooked wild rice	1/2 tsp. tarragon
5 Tbsp. butter	1/2 tsp. salt
3 Tbsp. shallot or whites of	pepper
scallions, finely chopped	1 Tbsp. brandy or sherry

Follow the cooking directions for wild rice printed on the package. A generous 1/2 cup of raw wild rice will yield 2 cups of cooked rice.

Slice 1/2 pound of mushrooms on the large blade of a vegetable grater. Heat 3 tablespoons of butter in a large skillet until it begins to spatter. Sauté the mushrooms for 3 minutes, stirring often. Remove to a large bowl, using a rubber scraper to get everything.

Heat 2 more tablespoons of butter and sauté 3 tablespoons of finely chopped shallots or scallions and 1/2 cup of sliced almonds. Watch this carefully, for as soon as the almonds begin to brown, in about 1 minute, remove them and the shallots to the bowl.

Add 2 cups of cooked wild rice, 1/2 teaspoon each of salt and tarragon, and a few turns of the pepper mill. Moisten with a tablespoon of brandy or sherry. Mix everything thoroughly but do it by tossing lightly.

MUSHROOM BULGUR STUFFING

Stuffing for 5 or 6 pounds of poultry, meat, or fish

Follow the directions for Mushroom Kasha Stuffing and substitute one cup of uncooked bulgur wheat for the cup of groats. Two tablespoons of pine nuts (pignole) may be added with the onions and peppers.

DUXELLES STUFFING

Mushroom Duxelles makes the supreme stuffing. Dishes ranging all the way from the tiniest hors d'oeuvre tartlette to the largest turkey become more festive when duxelles is added. The following recipe is one which every serious cook should be able to prepare for special occasions.

Mushroom Duxelles (see Index) can always be made in advance. The general rule for duxelles stuffing is equal amounts of duxelles and bread crumbs (or cooked rice). However, any variation is possible, such as 2 cups of large crumbs to 1 cup duxelles or vice versa. No other ingredients are necessary except for some liquid, such as wine or stock, to moisten the stuffing. The seasoning is in the duxelles.

If a delicate fish, such as rainbow trout, or a rare bird, such as squab or partridge, is to be stuffed, the duxelles can be used as is and should be packed lightly.

Prepared duxelles can also be substituted for the sautéed mushrooms in the preceding stuffing recipes, although *substitute* is hardly the word.

VARIATIONS AND EXPANSIONS

Giblets:

Chop and sauté in butter for a few minutes. If the amount is greater than 1/2 cup, remove the same amount of bread or rice.

Don't wash or peel mushrooms. Wipe clean with fingers, or damp
paper towel. Cut a thin slice off the bottom of each stem.

Bread:

Any kind of bread may be used, corn, whole-wheat, rye, or rolls.

Truffles:

One or 2 finely chopped truffles can be added.

Seafood:

A cup of chopped oysters, clams, shrimp, etc., may be substituted for the same amount of bread or rice.

Fat:

The butter may be replaced by oil, chicken or bacon fat, or a combination.

Additional Seasonings:

Chives, paprika, basil, oregano, chopped nuts, chopped water chestnuts, cooked sausage meat, chopped ham, cooked crumbled bacon, chopped cooked prunes, raisins, olives, capers.

MUSHROOM DUXELLES

1 scant cup

The story goes that there was a 17th-century French nobleman, a Marquis d'Uxelles, who was a great gastronome. Even greater was his chef, La Varenne, who is credited with being the first to depart from the Italian methods of cooking which had been imported by Catherine de Médicis. In 1651 his *Le Cuisinier Français* was published. It was the first clear and systematic cookbook to appear. La Varenne was the first chef to use mushrooms in the manner now known, in honor of his master, as duxelles.

Duxelles is a classic ingredient in cooking. It means mushrooms chopped fine and sautéed in butter, seasoned, rather dry. Duxelles is used to enhance other dishes. For this purpose, it is prepared in advance and kept on hand. Duxelles recipes usually require the juice of the mushrooms to be squeezed out at the start. The following recipe does not, because flavor is lost that way. The moisture is steamed out in cooking.

Mushroom Duxelles is chiefly used in sauces or as a stuffing or along with other ingredients as stuffing. It is an incomparable filling for rainbow trout and partridge. One of the most distinctive dinner party dishes is Filet of Beef Wellington, a whole tenderloin of beef surrounded with duxelles and rolled in crust (see Index). Many of the elaborate garnishes in *haute cuisine* use Mushroom Duxelles for filling artichoke bottoms, tomato cases, pastry shells, etc.

Having Mushroom Duxelles at hand in the refrigerator can stimulate the creation of new mushroom dishes. Some examples for using it follow, but try a spoon or two in whatever you happen to be fixing, such as scrambled eggs, a soup, or a vegetable.

1/2 lb. mushrooms	1/2 tsp. salt
2 shallots or 1 onion	1/8 tsp. pepper
3 Tbsp. butter	1 Tbsp. chopped parsley
2 Tbsp. finely chopped ham	

Don't wash or peel mushrooms. Wipe clean with fingers, or damp paper towel. Cut a thin slice off the bottom of each stem.

Chop $1/2$ pound of mushrooms very fine. This can easily be done by putting the mushrooms through a meat grinder, using the medium blade. Or the mushrooms can be sliced on the large blade of a vegetable grater and then chopped. If a meat grinder is used, put 2 shallots (or an onion) through too. Otherwise, chop the shallots (or onion) fine.

In a large skillet melt 3 tablespoons of butter over moderately high heat and cook the mushrooms and shallots (or onion) for 8 minutes. Keep stirring so that as much steam as possible will escape. Add $1/2$ teaspoon of salt, $1/8$ teaspoon of pepper, a tablespoon of freshly chopped parsley, and 2 tablespoons of finely chopped ham. Stir. The mushroom pieces will no longer lump together, but will be separated.

Instead of ham, some cooks season Mushroom Duxelles with nutmeg or tomato sauce. Or they add wine or stock, which is reduced and disappears. Duxelles can be kept in the refrigerator for at least a week in a tightly covered container. It also freezes well.

DUXELLES DIP

Spoon $1/2$ cup or more of cooled Mushroom Duxelles into a pint of sour cream.

DUXELLES SPREAD

Soften $1/2$ pound of cream cheese with a little milk or cream and add $1/2$ cup or more of Mushroom Duxelles.

DUXELLES BUTTER

Allow $1/4$ pound of sweet butter to soften at room temperature. Cream 3 tablespoons of Mushroom Duxelles into it. This makes a fine base for spreading on canapés or finger sandwiches.

MUSHROOM BREAD

2 loaves

A cookbook without bread is like a tree without leaves: naked. Naturally, this recipe uses mushrooms, and, as you might guess, it's great.

½ lb. mushrooms
1 cup milk
2 Tbsp. butter
2 Tbsp. sugar
1 Tbsp. salt

1 cup warm water
2 packages dry yeast
6 cups flour
2 Tbsp. chopped shallots or
  onions

In a small saucepan scald 1 cup of milk. Remove from heat and add 2 tablespoons of butter, 2 tablespoons of sugar, and a tablespoon of salt. Mix.

In a cup of warm water dissolve 2 packages of active dry yeast. Stir with a spoon and when it is dissolved pour it into a large bowl. Pour the milk into the bowl too.

Measure 3 cups of flour and sift into the bowl. Stir with a wooden spoon. Measure 2 more cups of flour and sift into the bowl.

Don't wash or peel mushrooms. Wipe clean with fingers, or damp paper towel. Cut a thin slice off the bottom of each stem.

Use the spoon to stir a little, then discard it and use your hands to incorporate the flour into the dough.

Sprinkle a board with some flour and knead the dough with the heels of your hands until it is satiny and elastic. Place the dough in a buttered bowl and turn it so the top is buttered. Cover with a towel and place in a warm spot (over a pilot light is good) and allow it to double in bulk, about 1 hour.

Punch the dough down and knead a little in the bowl. Slice 1/2 pound of mushrooms on the large blade of a vegetable grater and chop a little. Finely chop 2 tablespoons of shallots or onion and knead them into the dough along with the mushrooms. Knead them in gradually, a handful at a time. This is best done in the bowl until all the mushroom pieces are incorporated. The mushrooms will make the dough much moister than it was, and quite sticky.

Sprinkle 1/2 cup of flour onto the board and knead the dough some more. As the flour becomes used, add more from the remaining 1/2 cup. You may not use it all, but while kneading, you will use most of it. This is rather hard work but it only lasts about 5 minutes. The kneading helps the texture and gets rid of air bubbles. Allow the dough to rest while you butter 2 loaf pans.

Cut the dough in half and shape into 2 rectangles. Place them in the buttered loaf pans and brush the tops with butter. You can pat them in to fit nicely. Place in a warm spot and allow them to rise for about 1/2 hour. Bake in a preheated 375° oven for 45 minutes. Remove from the pans to cool on a rack.

MUSHROOM BISCUITS

12 to 15 biscuits

If you like biscuits and you like mushrooms, you'll be crazy about mushroom biscuits. Use them for creamed chicken—in a mushroom sauce, of course. Or just eat them as you would any other biscuits.

4 medium mushrooms	1 Tbsp. baking powder
2 cups all-purpose flour	5 Tbsp. butter
1 tsp. salt	2/3 cup milk

Measure 2 cups of all-purpose flour. Sift with 1 teaspoon of salt and 1 tablespoon of baking powder into a bowl. Add 5 tablespoons of chilled butter and cut it into the flour with a pastry blender or two knives until the texture is consistently coarse throughout, not lumpy or chunky.

Shred the mushrooms over the flour-butter mixture. Stir with a fork. Add 2/3 cup of milk and stir some more. Knead the dough in the bowl by rolling it to get all the flour and mushrooms from the sides.

On a lightly floured board pat dough out smooth to 1/2-inch thickness. Cut with a biscuit cutter or an inverted water glass dipped in very little flour. Place on a buttered baking sheet and bake in a preheated 450° oven for 12 to 15 minutes.

These biscuits freeze well before baking as well as after baking.

Don't wash or peel mushrooms. Wipe clean with fingers, or damp paper towel. Cut a thin slice off the bottom of each stem.

FLUTING MUSHROOMS

Fluting is to mushrooms as make-up is to a beautiful woman. A magnificent dish is enhanced when garnished with mushrooms; it is adorned when the mushrooms are fluted. The late Louis Diat of the Ritz put it in perfect gastronomic language: "Nothing proclaims the experience and skill of a chef so surely as a beautifully 'turned' mushroom, blooming like a flower on top of a beef filet or a baked fish."

Americans do not have to go to the most expensive restaurants to dine in great luxury these days. We can do it at home. The ingredients for some of the finest dishes in the world are available on the shelves of most supermarkets. This abundance, plus the excellent cookbooks now being published and the fact that America is a do-it-yourself nation, permits the home cook to approximate the cuisine of the fine restaurant chef.

Fluted mushrooms are sometimes referred to as "turned" because one turns the mushroom to make the grooves. They are also called "grooved" or "channeled" and are described as pinwheel-like in design. Fluting requires practice, but it is not too difficult for the serious cook. The overall effect is worth the effort.

For best results work with large, firm, white, very fresh mushrooms with closed caps. If the mushrooms are more than a few days old, the outer layer of skin becomes rubbery and offers resistance to the knife blade.

HOW TO FLUTE

Materials:

1. A bowl containing 2 cups of water and 2 tablespoons of lemon juice.
2. A small, sharp, pointed paring knife.
3. A tall thin glass, jar, or juice can with water and a tablespoon of lemon juice.

Preparation:

1. Cut the stems. Don't remove them by jerking to one side. If the mushrooms are to be used directly on meat or fish, or under glass, cut the stem flush with the underside of the cap. If the mushrooms are to be placed in parsley or other greens, cut the stem $1/2$ inch from the cap, thus providing it with a pedestal.
2. Dip the mushroom into the bowl of lemon-water before fluting. Dip the knife into the jar of lemon-water before each cut. Lemon-water keeps the mushroom white. If the cap starts to stain a light brownish color from handling, don't worry—the stain will bleach out while the finished mushroom sits in the bowl of lemon-water.

Technique:

A mushroom becomes fluted because it is turned on the blade of a sharp knife. Two turns are necessary to make each groove or channel. The groove is not cut by sawing the knife into the mushroom, but by turning the mushroom itself. Some cooks find it easier to turn the mushroom toward them, rather than away from them. Individual dexterity differs. Some fluters grasp the knife closer to the tip than others. Facility at this sort of thing has to do with balance.

Procedure:

Hold the mushroom in your left hand, your thumb on the top of the cap and your first or middle finger (whichever is more comfortable) on the stem. Hold the handle of the knife in your right hand with the sharp edge of the blade toward you. Place the point of the knife, almost touching your left thumb, on the top center of the mushroom and turn the mushroom counterclockwise, away from you, until the cut reaches the edge of the cap. Dip the knife. Complete the groove by making another cut directly behind the first one. For this, hold the blade at a sharper angle. In this way a curved 1/8- or 1/16-inch, moon-shaped sliver will be removed. Dip the knife and continue around the mushroom. To keep fluted mushrooms from discoloring, place them in the bowl of lemon-water.

Canned, Frozen, and Dried

CANNED MUSHROOMS

Fresh mushrooms are always preferable, but canned ones may be substituted when the fresh are not available. As a general rule, when the recipes in this book call for 1/2 pound of mushrooms, a standard 4-ounce can of buttons, slices, or stems and pieces may be used instead.

The best way to get the most flavor from canned mushrooms is to begin by draining them in a strainer. After they have drained, dry them on paper towels. They can't actually be dried but the surface liquid may be absorbed. Melt 2 tablespoons of butter in a skillet and add about one tablespoon or more of finely chopped shallots, scallions, or onions. Cook the mushrooms with the onions for about 3 minutes, stirring often. Add salt and pepper. The canned liquid is excellent for soups, sauces, and as a stock for cooking vegetables.

FROZEN MUSHROOMS

Commercially frozen whole mushrooms may be used as a substitute for fresh ones. They are packaged either in plastic bags or in standard vegetable cartons. The number of mushrooms contained in a package is usually printed on the label. The general rule to follow for using them in the recipes in this book is: 1/2 pound of fresh mushrooms is about 12 medium-size ones; use the same number of frozen mushrooms. Do not try to substitute by weight.

Frozen whole mushrooms are best when used in soups, sauces, and with other foods, rather than by themselves as sautéed mushrooms. They can, however, be sautéed and then combined successfully with other cooked food. They are easier to handle when partially defrosted. Frozen mushrooms should not be completely thawed before using.

HOME FREEZING

Mushrooms freeze very well when they are sliced, chopped, or ground and cooked with other foods. When prepared in this way and frozen, they are excellent and can be kept for as long as a year. Some examples are Mushroom Sauces, Soups, Meat Loaf, Bread and Biscuits, Quenelles, Butter, Chili, Duxelles, and Gumbo.

Thinly sliced sautéed mushrooms can be kept for about six months. This is a good freezer investment. They can be sautéed and packed in sandwich-size plastic bags, ready to use for quick enrichment of a dish. Since they are thinly sliced, they defrost almost immediately when stirred into a boiling pot.

Fluted mushrooms may be frozen also, but not quite as successfully. Diners do not always eat the fluted mushrooms on cold platters, and if they were especially well-executed, it's a shame not to use them again. I freeze them and they look just as pretty the second time but taste heavier.

Whole sautéed mushrooms can be frozen and are fine if used along with other foods.

Home freezing of raw mushrooms may be done, but it is not as successfully accomplished as commercial freezing. The commercial technique of the quick freeze requires more elaborate equipment than is found in home kitchens. I freeze them and they are all right if used before they have thawed, and are combined with other cooked foods. One month is the maximum time to store whole fresh mushrooms in a freezer. They don't spoil after that, but their lovely texture disintegrates.

All frozen foods should be placed in airtight containers allowing some room for expansion. Glass jars with screw-top lids are good for freezing mushroom sauces. Be sure to leave 1/2-inch air space at the top.

Uncooked mushroom hamburgers freeze well. They should be packed with wax paper between each patty and then placed in an airtight plastic container. To separate the hamburgers for easy defrosting, hit the edge of the frozen patties on the edge of a table,

Don't wash or peel mushrooms. Wipe clean with fingers, or damp paper towel. Cut a thin slice off the bottom of each stem.

and they will separate. They may be cooked while still frozen, and are practical to have on hand because a single hamburger is always available, ready to cook.

DRIED MUSHROOMS

If you are not familiar with the taste of dried mushrooms, you're in for a marvelous new gastronomic experience. Their flavor, though subtle, is unmistakable. There is a suggestion of early morning woods about the taste they bring to foods they are cooked with.

Only a few varieties of dried wild mushrooms are available commercially. The most common one is the cep (*Boletus edulis*) and next is the Oriental *shiitake* (*Lentinus edodes*). All dried mushrooms must be soaked before cooking. It is not necessary to wash them before soaking. They will drip sand or soil during the soaking process. The mushrooms should be removed from the water they were soaked in. That water may be strained through a strainer lined with a paper towel. The mushroom water will be an asset when added to any dish, the one those mushrooms are used in or any other.

Whole dried mushrooms that were fleshy and thick when fresh, like the cep, require three hours of soaking time. If separated, caps and stems need only two hours. Pieces and thin slices need only one hour, as do the Oriental whole mushroom caps, which are altogether more delicate.

Two ounces of dried mushrooms soaked in $1\frac{1}{2}$ cups of water will yield $1\frac{1}{3}$ cups of chopped mushrooms and liquid.

Always use at least 1 cup of water to soak 1 ounce of mushrooms. For 2 or 3 ounces, use $1\frac{1}{2}$ cups of water and for 4, 5, or 6 ounces, use 2 cups of water.

After the correct amount of soaking time, dried mushrooms can be used in dishes with fresh mushrooms or as a flavoring by themselves. They can withstand longer cooking without detriment and can be added to a sauce, stew, or soup at the beginning of the cooking period. It is a good idea to soak and boil them and keep in the refrigerator in a tightly covered container to have available to add to various dishes. They will keep in the refrigerator for several days.

It is hard to make a rule for cooking dried wild mushrooms, for so much depends upon the size, as well as the fleshiness, of the mushroom when it was fresh. In general, however, the Oriental variety, which seems to be sold only in Oriental food shops, needs 10 to 15 minutes of cooking, including whole, unbroken caps, after the soaking period. All others, including the types found in supermarkets, should be cooked at least 20 minutes if they are broken into pieces or if they are sliced. If the pieces are large, or if whole caps are used, at least 30 minutes cooking time will be required after the soaking period.

Mushroom powder, found on herb and spice shelves, is a versatile condiment and can be used with scarcely any cooking at all. For example, sprinkling it on hamburgers just before they are removed from the heat is enough to bring out full mushroom flavor. Mushroom powder can be added to rice for the entire cooking time. Altogether, mushroom powder is a handy thing to have around the kitchen. It adds style to all sorts of ordinary dishes.

Wild Mushrooms
and Truffles

WILD MUSHROOMS

Wild mushrooms are very different from the cultivated ones. Their flavor is much more distinctive; there is an added richness that comes from the complex underground plant growth which takes place long before the actual fruit, the fungus, emerges.

It is because of their unique, delectable flavor that such a fuss has surrounded eating wild mushrooms. This has been going on for centuries. There are even words in the ancient Chaldean language to distinguish the varieties.

Because fresh wild mushrooms are rarely sold in the United States, we are generally not as familiar with them as we are with the commercial, cultivated, white umbrella-type mushroom (*Agaricus campestris*). In many cities and towns in Europe wild mushrooms are sold in the markets, as are the cultivated ones. The two most common varieties being the cep (*Boletus edulis*) and the chanterelle (*Cantharellus cibarius*). Both have long growing seasons and tend to be less perishable than other mushrooms.

Because stores don't sell them doesn't mean we can't enjoy these magnificent fungi. There are two ways: the more expensive is to go to an elegant mid-town Manhattan restaurant in the spring or fall and order them; the other—and better—way is to pick them yourself. If the idea appeals to you, but you haven't considered it before, then perhaps this is the time to do so. The first qualification for becoming a mushroom hunter is to be a responsible person. Smart alecks don't qualify. That is not to say one must be a botanist or a mycologist to enjoy mushrooms. Anyone who is interested and willing to give the whole idea some serious attention and a little study can do it. There is no mushroom mystique; there are only facts. It is my hope that this chapter will act as a stimulating introduction.

Those who are interested, but are not ready to go out into the field, should not be put off by sensational stories about toadstools, hallucinations, and possible poisoning. The facts simply do not support such gross exaggerations. There are well over a hundred edible and choice mushrooms to choose from among the more than two thousand varieties of fungi which grow in the United States. Many edible mushrooms are not recommended because their taste isn't especially interesting. As for the destructive ones, there are only a handful, and they are easily recognized. There are five guide points of identification: cap, gills or pores, stem, ring, and cup. These are clearly laid out by the guidebooks. Only the most reckless novice would ignore the rules of the game and mistake them.

As curious as it may sound, the best place to begin an acquaintance with wild mushrooms is your own supermarket. Start out by buying some mushroom powder, made of dried wild mushrooms. You'll find it on the herb and spice shelves. If your store doesn't carry it try another, for there are at least five large companies packing it these days. Sprinkle some on a hamburger, on eggs, on rice or mashed potatoes to familiarize your taste buds with this new refinement. Try a package or two of the dried mushrooms sold in little cellophane bags and in round plastic containers. Put some in a soup, stew, or sauce. Look through the envelopes of dehydrated soups; some contain imported wild mushrooms.

If you still need more warming up before going into the field, buy a can of wild mushrooms. Large department stores and fancy food shops carry them. They are expensive, admittedly, but a dollar or two spent this way might put you on the trail of a new and most worthwhile pleasure.

The wild mushrooms most frequently available in cans are the same ones which are most popularly sold in Europe, the cep (*Boletus edulis*) and the chanterelle (*Cantharellus cibarius*). They are imported from various places and though they are labeled in their country of origin, the Latin nomenclature is usually given as well. A can usually has a picture of the mushrooms it contains. Some of the names you might come across on a can of ceps are:

cèpe	France
steinpilz	Germany and Switzerland
herrenpilz	Austria
porcino	Italy

Don't wash or peel mushrooms. Wipe clean with fingers, or damp paper towel. Cut a thin slice off the bottom of each stem.

baroviki	Poland
belya-grib	Russia
stensopp	Denmark

The chanterelles are imported mostly from France and Switzerland and the common name is the same in both countries, *chanterelle,* although the French also call this mushroom *girolle.* Occasionally, there are some German cans with the name *pfefferling,* and on Swedish ones, it is *vanlig kantarell.*

Simply sauté the canned wild ceps for the purest flavor. Drain the mushrooms in a strainer and save the liquid they were packed in for enhancing the taste of another vegetable, or for a sauce. Lay the ceps on paper towels, pat them dry, and separate the stems. Slice the stems and sauté them in butter over moderately high heat for 5 minutes. Add the caps, sliced, and sauté for 5 more minutes. Sprinkle with salt and pepper.

The chanterelles get different treatment. Slice them, stems included, and steam them in butter in a covered skillet, using low heat, for 15 minutes.

When you start picking the nutty-flavored ceps and the spicy, apricot-flavored chanterelles yourself, your culinary repertoire can expand to great heights of sophistication and elegance: To stuff a bird with wild rice and wild mushrooms and cover all with a wine sauce of the same wild mushrooms is to revel in nature's gifts to man.

Before wild mushrooms can be cooked, however, they have to be found. A basic rule for beginners is: *Know* what you are searching for. Guessing is not allowed. You *must* use guidebooks. The titles at the end of this chapter should be helpful in surveying the guidebooks available. The pamphlet *Some Common Edible and Poisonous Mushrooms of Pennsylvania* is free and I urge everyone to send for it. The mushrooms described, with clear photographs, are by no means limited to the state of Pennsylvania, so don't let that detail in the title keep you from ordering it.

It is wisest at the start to learn to identify only a couple of mushrooms and limit yourself to picking those. Don't be overambitious and try to learn them all at once. When you collect mushrooms, keep each species separate, preferably in paper bags. Dig up the entire mushroom, for if there is a cup at the base of the stem, that is a significant point of identification. Select only choice specimens. If they look overripe or have been discovered by insects before your discovery, don't pick them.

By the way, mushrooms can cause allergic reactions for some people. But so can eggs, chocolate, and strawberries.

The 5 varieties discussed are not only choice but are reasonably common. There is nothing questionable, esoteric, or rare about them.

CEPS

We'll start with the cep (*Boletus edulis*) because it is the most familiar wild mushroom. The guidebooks use such words as fleshy, rotund, swollen, thick, and solid to describe the cep. The cap is brown in shade and varies from chocolate malted to a dark brown, or if it is growing in direct sunlight, there can be a reddish cast to the brown. This mushroom is found on the ground, usually in pine woods, sometimes among beeches, and also in sandy soil if there are pines around.

On the underside of the cap, instead of gills (as in the cultivated mushrooms we buy) there are pores which look spongy, or like a lot of crowded pinholes. These are a layer of fine tubes very close together which run vertically from the cap. The little holes, which are the openings of these tubes, give a porous look to this undersurface. In the button stage of growth these tubes are white, and as the mushroom develops to maturity, they become yellowish. When overripe the tubes finally turn a yellowish green. The cap is smooth and rounded and averages from 3 to 8 inches across. The flesh of the cep is always white, thick, and firm when fresh, and will not change color if broken or cut. Other varieties in the bolete family do change color.

A distinguishing characteristic of this mushroom is its bulbous bottom. The stem gradually thickens at the base. In proportion to the cap, the stem is short and swollen and from 2 to 5 inches in height. The cep never has a thin stem. The stem is always many shades lighter than the cap, usually beige, and is ornamented with a raised network of lines on the upper, narrower portion. This minute reticulation of fine veins is more often than not quite discernible, for they are in slight relief and either a shade lighter or darker than the stem. But this is not always so; sometimes these lines are the exact shade of the stem, making it harder for the naked eye to see. Look very closely.

The cep season is a generous one, lasting through the summer and well into autumn. The cep has no distinctive smell. When tasted in the field, this mushroom is sweet and nutty.

Refrigerate your mushrooms as soon as you get home if you're not going to cook them right away. They are best when eaten the day they are gathered. As you pick them, before placing them in a paper bag, trim their stems at the bottom with a knife and remove as much gross dirt as possible. Don't wash them until you're ready to use them. Rinse under cold running water, round side up, so the pores don't fill up with water, and rub any soil off with your fingers. Dry them on paper towels. Do not peel.

If your ceps are very large, give the stems some extra cooking, for they'll be quite a bit tougher than the caps. However, in the button stage you can cook stems and caps together. Some cooks remove the tubes, or fleshy pores, on the underside of the cap. I don't unless the cep is so mature that upon touching it, the tubes fall away. The tubes are a delicious and integral part of the cap.

Sauté in butter and olive oil for quickest cooking—10 minutes for the stems, sliced, and 5 minutes for the caps, sliced. Because of the firmness of this mushroom, it is marvelous stuffed. Use any of the Stuffed Mushrooms recipes and add 5 more minutes cooking time. The cep can be used for any of the recipes in this book; just remember to add the additional 5 minutes.

CHANTERELLES

The chanterelle (*Cantharellus cibarius*) is very different from the cep in color, flavor, and appearance and must be cooked a little longer. This fungus is a beautiful sight when one comes upon it in the forest: golden trumpets growing from the earth. At maturity they look like cornucopias. They are frequently found in groups under hardwoods and conifers.

The egg-yellow color is uniform in cap and stem. There is practically no point of distinction between the two, for the cap runs into the stem like a funnel. The gills of the chanterelle are not really gills but are narrow folds, heavier, thicker, and more widely spaced than

gills. They branch and fork and continue down the stem, which becomes thinner at its base. The stem may be from 1 to 3 inches long. These non-gills, or folds, can be slightly paler or slightly darker than the rest of the mushroom. The smooth cap of a young chanterelle is at first convex, then gradually flattens out; at maturity a depression appears in the center. The cap measures from 2 to 4 inches in diameter and has a wavy or lobed margin with the edges appearing to be rolled under. The firm flesh is white or very pale yellow and smells of fragrant apricots.

The slightly peppery but agreeable flavor of the chanterelle is responsible for its German name, *pfefferling*. Like the cep, this mushroom is sold fresh in the markets of Europe. The season for it is July and August, and sometimes part of September.

Chanterelles keep their beautiful color when cooked, but shrink more than other fungi. Their flavor is so distinctive that they should be served as a separate dish. High heat will toughen them, therefore cook them gently. My favorite method, especially if the yield has been small, or if they are the first of the season, is the following:

In a skillet sauté some shallots or the whites of scallions in quite a bit of butter until they are softened but not browned. Slice the chanterelles lengthwise in halves or quarters and let them steam, covered, with the shallots or scallions and some lemon juice ($\frac{1}{2}$ lemon for $\frac{1}{2}$ pound chanterelles). Cook over a low flame for 15 minutes. They will release their own liquid.

For a special treat serve chanterelles in Velvet Mushroom Sauce (see Index). Follow the sauce recipe but prepare the chanterelles as above and add them to the sauce at the end with $\frac{1}{2}$ teaspoon of tarragon. Eliminate the tablespoon of lemon juice in the sauce recipe.

PUFFBALLS

Another distinct and easily recognized species is the puffball (*Calvatia gigantea* and *Calvatia cyathiformis*). Some mycologists consider this the best mushroom for beginners to start with. The spherical shape cannot be mistaken and is easily spotted, for it grows on the ground in low meadows or in well-drained soil, usually in open places. There is no cap or stem; it has the shape of a ball, a puffball.

The meadow puffballs (*Calvatia cyathiformis*) average between 2 and 4 inches and are somewhat pear-shaped in the early stages while the gigantic ones (*Calvatia gigantea*) can be over a foot wide and weigh 15 to 20 pounds. These spherical mushrooms are attached to their underground plants by a rootlike cord. When young, a puffball has a very smooth, firm skin. As it matures, the outer skin begins to crack and fall away. The flesh is white, smooth, homogeneous, and has a springiness to the touch. When it is cut, the interior should be without blemish or color—even a tinge of yellow means that the mushroom is past maturity and its delicate flavor will be marred with bitterness. As the puffball ages, its interior changes color and it becomes slimy, then powdery. Their season is late summer and early fall.

Preparing the puffball for cooking is simple. No cleaning: peel it and the white firm flesh is ready to slice. It is so tender that it is used uncooked in salad. Although it isn't necessary, I like to marinate the slices in French dressing for about half an hour before combining with greens. Some mushroom eaters say the puffball has a taste similar to that of eggplant but I disagree; it is more subtle and at the same time has a wild pungency.

There is a lavishness which goes with cooking the puffball because it can be handled in large pieces. This feeling of abundance sometimes works in a negative way because many cooks overseason and overcook it. Be warned, restrain yourself. Your culinary prowess in the case of the puffball will best be demonstrated by bringing out its delicate flavor instead of submerging it with bread crumbs and herbs and spices.

Cut your white sphere into $1/2$-inch slices and sauté in half butter and half olive oil for about 4 minutes, using moderate heat. Turn. While the uncooked side is sautéeing, sprinkle with a little chervil, a little nutmeg, and salt and pepper.

To serve with a sauce, prepare the puffballs as directed here and use the chicken broth recipe, Basic Sauce II in the Sauce chapter.

The puffball is very good cut in pieces as for French fries—and prepared just that way. Vegetable oil for cooking should be very hot and the mushroom strips should be immersed for only a few minutes and quickly removed to paper towels. The heat of the oil immediately seals the puffball against the absorption of the fat. Sprinkle with salt.

MORELS

If it were ever necessary to justify developing an interest in mushrooms, the morel (*Morchella esculenta*) would be that justification. For me, it is the supreme mushroom. The morel is to fungi what *Le Montrachet* is to white wine, and by the way, they complement each other marvelously.

The morel is also called the sponge mushroom. It grows in the ground. It is from 2 to 6 inches high and has a broad stalk with an enlarged upper portion called a head or cap. This cap is unmistakable, for it is irregularly pitted like a honeycomb. These pits form small, cuplike structures and range in color from light gray-brown to deeper, tawny shades of brown. The stem is many shades lighter.

As this fungus ages, it becomes paler in color.

Because the morel is hollow through stem and cap, quite a number of them are needed to make a good portion. There are a few other varieties of morels which are very closely related to the *Morchella esculenta* and are equally good. If the shape of their cap is more or less rounded, conical, or oval and if it is deeply pitted, they are the same family; pick them. If you come upon some which at first look like morels but have wrinkled or convoluted caps, with an almost brainlike configuration, they are false morels. Beginners should leave them alone. Some people eat them and others do not.

Morels grow in a variety of places, such as old orchards, burned-over meadows, in woods, and along roadsides. Although they are not consistently found in groups, if you come upon one, it is likely that close scrutiny of the area will yield more specimens. The season is about two or three weeks in April and May but several crops may appear during that short period. Once you know their hiding places, you can return year after year and—if there has been enough rain—find them again.

Before cooking, morels must be washed thoroughly, for the pits can hold sand. Place them in a strainer, and the strainer in a pot. Let cold water run over them, lifting the strainer a few times, and then run more cold water over them. Never soak. Three minutes should be ample for the job. Use your fingers to wipe the stems.

Lay the mushrooms on a dish towel to dry. Pick up the ends of the towel and swing it very gently to move the mushrooms around, thereby getting rid of as much water as possible.

Morels are, of course, marvelous sautéed in butter and need only 5 minutes cooking time, when the large ones are halved lengthwise and the small ones are left whole. Sprinkle with a few drops of lemon juice, some chopped fresh parsley, and salt and pepper.

The hollow interior of morels might almost have been designed for stuffing. One good stuffing uses a cup of chopped, cooked chicken or a cup of ground veal which has been sautéed only long enough to remove the raw look. Add 1/4 cup bread crumbs, an egg, 1/4 cup milk or cream, a dash of nutmeg, and 1/4 teaspoon of marjoram. Mix well. Cut the morels in half the long way, including the stems; stuff one half and cover with the other. Place the stuffed morels in a well-buttered baking pan and line them up so that they are almost touching. Don't use too big a pan because the mushrooms must remain moist. Pour a little chicken broth in the baking pan and add a tablespoon of brandy. Dot each morel with butter. Cover and bake for 15 minutes in a preheated 375° oven. Serve this to the most demanding connoisseur and you will be applauded.

OYSTER MUSHROOM

Last in this group is a very common fungus, which also has a long season, the oyster mushroom (*Pleurotus ostreatus*). Some say the name comes from the flavor and others say it is derived from the shape. The oyster mushroom grows in clusters of fan- or shell-shaped caps on decaying trees, old stumps and trunks, and fallen logs. The overlapping caps, from 2 to 10 inches in diameter, are smooth and white in color—or light gray or grayish tan. The gills on the underside are white or a pale off-white. They are broad and rather far apart, fusing together as they extend down to the stem. The stem is difficult to see at first and sometimes doesn't even exist. When it does, it is short—under 2 inches—and often many stems of a crowded cluster unite at one base. The stem is rarely centered but is most frequently attached to the cap on one side. The flesh of the oyster mushroom is white and is best when it is soft and tender. If it feels tough, use only the outer parts, discarding the section close to the stem.

The oyster mushroom and its relatives usually grow in abundance; therefore by picking only the young, tender caps you can probably supply more than a single meal. This whole family is edible and a number of species are included in the same name. It fruits from early spring to very late fall. Use it for any of the recipes in this book.

The way I get the taste of oysters with this mushroom is by cooking it with okra. The texture, I guess, has something to do with it, for okra releases a gelatinous liquid. Cut the mushroom into 2-inch pieces. Sauté 2 scallions, including the green, in a couple of tablespoons of oil for 2 minutes. Add the mushroom pieces, some okra sliced in $1/2$-inch pieces, a slice of chopped boiled ham, some fresh chopped parsley, a pinch of dill weed, and salt and pepper. Cook over moderate heat for 15 minutes. Stir frequently. Serve with boiled rice.

I have purposely not discussed the common meadow mushroom (*Agaricus campestris*) which the mushroom hunter is likely to come upon in the field. Not that it isn't a fine tasting mushroom to carry home and cook; quite the contrary, the wild version of the

familiar cultivated one is most interesting. But I strongly feel that until one has carefully studied a few guidebooks, it is better to leave that one untouched.

Every book goes into detail about poisonous mushrooms. It is of great importance to know them. The most destructive mushroom may at first glance look like the meadow mushroom to the beginner; it is the *Amanita phalloides,* also known as the destroying angel, the deadly amanita, or the white death cap or cup. Although there are clear-cut distinctions between the amanita and the meadow mushroom, they may not appear obvious, particularly at the button stage of development, to the untutored eye.

This shouldn't dampen your enthusiasm, but only make you more careful. The five species described above have been carefully selected for their ease of identification. In spite of the lack of ambiguity concerning them, it is important to underline the point about the use of the guidebooks. Listed at the end of this chapter are some good ones to start with. With one or more of these in your pocket, you can join the distinguished world of mycophagy.

If you are very lucky and find more wild mushrooms than you can use in the few days after your hunt, you can preserve them. The best way to preserve mushrooms for an indefinite period of time is to dry them. Or they may be cooked fresh with other foods, particularly in sauces, and then frozen in airtight containers and kept for up to a year. Follow the directions for any of the mushroom sauces and just remember to give wild mushrooms some additional cooking time.

Stringing is a simple way to cope with a particularly large haul of oyster mushrooms, puffballs, or polypores. Cut the mushrooms into 2-inch pieces and string them with a needle and thread. Keep each piece separate from the next to allow full circulation of air. Then hang the strings in the shade, inside or out, to dry. They can be left that way until used. Never wash wild mushrooms before stringing them. Some people dry mushrooms in the sun and some in a slow oven. I myself do not think heat does mushrooms any good at all for drying.

All wild mushrooms, including morels, chanterelles, and ceps, can be strung. They can also be laid out to dry on a screen, without touching each other and with air circulating both top and bottom. When completely dry they can be stored.

To use dried wild mushrooms for cooking, soak them for 1 hour if they were 2 inches or less when fresh. If heavy boletes are strung and dried whole, including their rotund stems, they will need 3 hours of soaking.

Happy hunting and *bon appétit!*

TRUFFLES

Truffles are among the rarest of all gastronomic delicacies. In France truffle-hunting has gone on for centuries, particularly in the Périgord region, universally acknowledged as the best black truffle producing section of the world. The region is also known for geese with especially rich and large livers; put these both together and you have the main ingredients for the famous *pâté de foie gras.*

A truffle is an underground mushroom, usually found beneath oak and beech trees. They must be rooted out of the earth. For this purpose, truffle-hunters have trained female pigs and dogs (of either sex) to smell truffles from as much as 20 feet away and to root them out. If the hunter isn't quick, the truffle disappears.

Truffles are used as a flavoring for omelettes, pâtés, stuffing, and sauces, and as garnish. Their unique, pungent aroma permeates and distinctly flavors the food with which they come in contact. They also have a marvelous texture and are easy to handle.

There are two kinds of truffles on the market: the black and the white. (The whites are really gray or beige in color.) Both grow in France, but the Piedmont section of Italy is well known for the white variety. Both are fine tasting. However, it is taken for granted by most truffle eaters that the black variety is superior. The whites are in greater supply, making the blacks more expensive.

A small can, which usually contains no more than three truffles,

Don't wash or peel mushrooms. Wipe clean with fingers, or damp paper towel. Cut a thin slice off the bottom of each stem.

may be used to flavor many dishes. Sometimes canned truffles come peeled and sometimes not; if they are not, peel them very thinly and chop the peelings fine. They are perfectly good. More flavor is released from truffles if they sit, sliced, at room temperature in a spoon or two of Madeira or sherry for about half an hour before they are used.

There is a way to get extra use from them, too: place some thin slices on food in a tightly covered container in the refrigerator for 24 hours. The food will acquire the truffle flavor without even using the truffles. Truffles can be kept in the refrigerator for a full month, but they must be immersed in liquid, such as their own juice, oil, or wine. The canned ones don't have to be cooked, only heated through thoroughly so their volatility will be released. Canned truffles also freeze well.

There are good and bad truffle years, just as there are good and bad wine years. As a result, the price of truffles varies. Currently, the prices for a small can range from 79¢ to $1.59.

Mushroom Guidebooks

The Mushroom Hunter's Field Guide. Alexander H. Smith. Revised and enlarged 1964. University of Michigan Press, Ann Arbor, Mich. 312 pages. 188 species. 243 black and white photographs, 89 color plates. $6.95. (The most important, and therefore at the head of this otherwise alphabetical list.)

Field Book of Common Mushrooms. William S. Thomas. G. P. Putnam's Sons. New York, London, 1948. 369 pages. Profusely illustrated. $5.

*Fungi.** Elizabeth J. Moore and Verne N. Rockcastle. Cornell Science Leaflet, Volume 56, Number 3, March 1963. Mailing Room, Stone Hall, Cornell University, Ithaca, N.Y. 14850. 32 pages. 28 photographs. 25¢.

Mushrooms and Other Common Fungi of the San Francisco Bay Region. Robert T. and Dorothy B. Orr. University of California Press. Berkeley and Los Angeles, 1962. 71 pages. Many black and white drawings, 25 color photographs. Soft covers. $1.50.

The Observer's Book of Common Fungi. E. M. Wakefield. Frederick Warne & Co., Ltd. London, New York, 1958. 118 pages. Profusely illustrated. $1.25.

The Savory Wild Mushroom. Margaret McKenny. University of Washington Press. Seattle, 1962. 133 pages. Profusely illustrated, many photographs in full color. Soft covers. $3.95.

Some Common Edible and Poisonous Mushrooms. H. M. Fitzpatrick and W. W. Ray. New York State College of Agriculture. Mailing Room, Stone Hall, Cornell University, Ithaca, N.Y. 14850. Cornell Extension Bulletin 386, January 1963. 16 pages. 13 photographs. Free to New York state residents. 10¢ to others.

Some Common Edible and Poisonous Mushrooms of Pennsylvania. Charles L. Fergus. Penn State University, College of Agriculture, University Park, Penn. Bulletin 667, April 1964. 28 pages. 61 photographs. Free.

Some Common Mushrooms and How to Know Them. Vera K. Charles. U.S. Department of Agriculture, Superintendent of

*Not a guidebook in the usual sense but a very good introduction to the study of fungi in spite of its being written for young students.

Documents, U. S. Printing Office, Washington, D.C. 20402. Circular 143, July 1953. 60 pages. 48 illustrations. 25¢.

Some Edible Mushrooms and How to Cook Them. Nina Lane Faubion. Binfords and Mort, Portland, Oregon, 1938. Reprinted 1964. 198 pages. Illustrated. $3.95.

Twenty Common Mushrooms and How to Cook Them. George Coffin and Margaret Lewis, International Pocket Library, Bruce Humphries, Inc., Boston, Mass., 1965. 96 pages. Paper cover. Illustrated. 75¢.

Index